LOOK ME IN THE EYE

EXPANDED EDITION

LOOK ME IN THE EYE

Old Women Aging and Ageism

Barbara Macdonald
with Cynthia Rich

spinsters book company
SAN FRANCISCO

Published 1983. Second edition 1991.

First printing
10-9-8-7-6-5-4-3-2-1

Spinsters Book Company
P.O. Box 410687
San Francisco, CA 94141

Cover photos: Avery McGinn
Cover design: Pam Wilson Design Studio
Production: Elizabeth Brodersen, Linda Catalano, Theresa Gradine, Joan Meyers, Kathleen Wilkinson, Jenny Worley
Typeset in Goudy Oldstyle by Community Press, San Francisco and by Joan Meyers

Spinsters' desktop publishing system made possible by a grant from the Horizons Foundation-Bay Area Career Women Fund and by individual donors.

Library of Congress Cataloging in Publication Data

Macdonald, Barbara, 1912 or 13-
Look me in the eye : old women, aging, and ageism / by Barbara Macdonald with Cynthia Rich. — 2nd ed.
p. cm.
ISBN 0-933216-87-4 : $8.95
1. Aged women. 2. Aged women—social conditions. 3. Aged women—Psychology. 4. Ageism. 5. Aging. 6. Old age. I. Rich, Cynthia. II. Title.
HQ1061.M23 1991
305.48'9—dc20 91-36595
CIP

Acknowledgments

With minor changes, these essays appeared in the following publications: *Broomstick*, *Equal Times*, *Gay Community News*, *New Women's Times*, *Sojourner*, *Trivia*, *Lesbian Ethics*, and *Women's Studies Quarterly*.

We are grateful to all of these publications, but special appreciation goes to Catherine Nicholson, Harriet Desmoines, and Susan Leigh Star, who, in 1979, devoted the entire issue of *Sinister Wisdom #10* to aging, and who opened a door for "Do You Remember Me?"

Table of Contents

Barbara's Introduction

My essays in this book were written between 1978 and 1983, although it feels to me as though I have been in the process of writing them since I was in my teens and that only the lack of time, of some leisure and some freedom from the anxiety of earning a living kept me from writing them earlier. Yet these essays are about growing old and I had little knowledge of "old" when I was in my late teens. But they are also about difference—about otherness—and all my life I have had to deal with difference, so old age does not come to me now as a stranger. In so many ways these are the same essays I would have written when I was young, only the metaphor has changed.

It happened that I felt my difference because I was a lesbian. But difference is something we have all dealt with in our lives—that struggle to follow our impulse, our own uniqueness, to know aloneness; and that desire to be like everyone else—not to stand out, but to belong.

In "Do You Remember Me?" I speak of that second chance—how no experience is really missed. And thus it seems to me that whether we choose it or not, age in our society gives us a second opportunity (or places the demand on us, if that is how it feels) to finally deal with our difference if we have not done so before; to move out of that safe harbor of acceptability.

For me, dealing with powerful difference came early, the more so because of the period in which I grew up. Being a lesbian, or indeed a woman, in the '20s was not what it is today. Kotex had not been invented. *The Well of Loneliness* had not been written. Freud had not been popularized yet, and the sexual molestation of young girls by men (which he denied in practice but at least acknowledged in theory) had not yet been labeled as sick. It was unrecognized by the adult world; at the very least, it was unspoken of, and there was nothing a child or young girl could do with the knowledge she had of the danger all around her.

But when I was sitting on the edge of my seat at the Saturday afternoon matinee watching the lady being tied to the railroad track by a black cloaked villain and being rescued by a colorless, self-effacing, mechanized robot of a man, even before I was old enough to read the subtitles, I knew I didn't want to be any of the three of them. I certainly didn't want to be the villain, and there was no way I wanted to be that silly woman, yelling Help, Help—to be rescued by that robot of a man I knew was no safer than the men my sister and I were very careful never to sit next to in a dark theater. I didn't have the word for it, but I was choosing then to be a lesbian and it was a choice I was to make many times in the next sixty years.

I have always been a lesbian—always loved women, gotten my strength and my sense of self from women. I was always in love. From four to eleven I fell in love with the teacher or the woman next door. This was viewed as a phase by my family but not by me; I knew. After eleven, I was hearing the all too familiar "I would rather you were dead" from my mother. My life of being the "other" had begun. I was not like anyone in my family. I was not like anyone in my school. I was not like anyone in my town.

When I was eighteen in a small college in Santa Ana, I fell in love with a young girl on campus and the relationship lasted for three years. It was in the spring of our last term, when we were making plans to leave this small community to go to Berkeley, that Barbara told her parents about her sexual relationship with me and the sky fell in. Her parents were active Christian Scientists; they threatened to have her put out of the church. The Dean of Women who had been my champion, who had taught me to write, and who had first helped me to get published, withdrew her public support of me as her protegée and went to the President of the college to have me expelled. The President called me in and gave me two choices: I could be expelled immediately; or on the other hand—he admitted he would like to avoid a scandal—if I would agree not to speak to the girl again, I could remain until the end of the term. I was paralyzed by the shock as Barbara had told me nothing and had in fact only told her parents the night before, and I had had no preparation for the scene I came on when I went to classes that morning—classes I found closed to me. I, at least, had the guts to agree to nothing, pointing out to the President that it was not a decision either he or I could make and that I would have to talk with Barbara to know what she wanted to do.

Barbara had been raised in that small town and had grown up on the same street where the Dean of Women lived. I was a stranger come to town with many strange ways: I did not live with my family , I earned my living by parachute jumping, I was a writer, I did not go to church. Now the lines were clearly drawn and Barbara was one of theirs, "hypnotized" by the stranger, the Dean said.

So when Barbara and I met on that spring afternoon near the tennis courts, the locust trees that only the day before bloomed to affirm us, today seemed never to have bloomed for me. We had been lovers, now we were strangers. She, crying and contrite, relieved that her life could go on the same, spoke of what it would mean to her and to her family if the church were closed to her. We agreed to comply. I was allowed to finish out the term, but the President stated clearly that my "homosexuality" would go into my academic file and folow me wherever I went. So for the rest of my life (for most of my life was academic) I never knew when I was identified as a lesbian and when I was not.

When I try to recall the years that followed that experience, all the years of feeling different, the memory of my fourteen years with Marge is like a lamp hanging in some archway of my life: it lets light back into the years before we met and the soft edges of its light reach ahead into my todays, illuminating a little even the dark years that followed our separation.

It was in Baltimore that we separated. The year Kennedy was assassinated. Somehow I always think of the two things together. I was overwhelmed by my loss. Once again, I was alone. I went to work every day to survive. I knew no one to whom I could talk. Mechanically, I performed the necessary daily tasks to go on living, while my loss went unrecognized by anyone in my daily surroundings. Yet on the other hand, there was this strange national mourning going on around me. I'm sure I would have felt worse if there had been some national celebration of joy going on instead. But the experience of having the reality of your own life—your joy or your grief—unconfirmed by the reality around you is to know that you are the "other" and that you must somehow chart your own course.

Since 1975, when for the first time I had the freedom to begin this work, much has happened. Cynthia and I met, came to live together, and to share our work and our view of our separate life experiences with twenty years' difference in our ages. For me this meant leaving an administrative job where friends and colleagues had known me since my mid-fifties. It meant moving to Cambridge a few blocks from Harvard Square, where to step out of the door was to step out into a world of young men ("promising" young men according to male standards of who and what is important and promising in the world) and no one is less promising, less important in that scene than an old woman. Again I was outside, again I was "other." Again I lived with the never-knowing when people would turn away from me, not because they had identified me as a lesbian, since I was no longer thought of as a sexual being, but because they had identified me as old. I had lived my life without novels, movies, radio, or television telling me that lesbians existed or that it was possible to be glad to be a lesbian. Now nothing told me that old women existed, or that it was possible to be glad to be an old woman. Again the silence held powerful and repressive messages. Again I had to chart my own course, this time into growing old. This time with Cynthia, who chose to explore with me both the process and the politics of aging.

At the time we met, the women's movement was affecting the lives of all women; many were freed by it, some were frightened by it. Our lives, Cynthia's and mine, were freed by it in deep and permanent ways. It has made this work possible, which we hope gives back to women some of the energy and vision that is our debt.

Cynthia's Introduction

It is September, 1974. I am 41. It is raining, a warm, steady rain. I have come into Cambridge to meet a woman. I know more about her than she knows about me. I know that she is 62, that years ago she entertained people as a parachute jumper because, even though it terrified her and she believed she would die, it was the only way to make money to buy books for college. I know that she had once worked pressing clothes in a laundry. I know that she is a social worker in Connecticut. I know that she is a feminist and a lesbian. I know these things because I have read her autobiographical submissions to my course, a workshop in Feminist Writing. I am very eager to have her join the workshop.

She is waiting under the awning of the pub where we were to meet. Through the rain I see her white, short, straight hair and the strong solidness of her body under the blue jacket.

"It's closed," she says. We hurry across the street to a little basement pub I know. We have a couple of beers and we talk, about the course, about her life, which she wants to write about. Her eyes are very blue, her gaze very direct. She tells me that she will be leaving the work world in another year or so, and now for the first time can tell the story of her life—as a woman and a lesbian—and know that she can find readers. But she fears that all those years of never being free to write will make her undisciplined. She talks about aging, not being able to believe it, not being able to deny it. She wants to write about that, too. Nothing she has read reflects her own experiences, of making love and later taking a shower, looking down and seeing that her hair is thinner; she can see the cleft she has not seen since she was ten years old. She decides to take the workshop.

We meet, by chance as it were, every Sunday night before the workshop in a brightly-lit deli around the corner from the school. We sit in a booth and talk for two hours, and the talking gives me energy for the week. More energy than the workshop, since I am not prepared for the stored up hunger of these women, their spoken, unspoken—and conflicting—needs, the intense mother-role that I am asked to play. It never occurs to me that in their eyes I am not only the workshop leader but, except for Barbara, fifteen years older than the oldest of them. In my own eyes, I am the perennial younger sister, never older than anyone. With Barbara, neither of us is the mother. Since I do not believe that teacher and student are meant to give to each other in exactly the same way, I learn more about her life than I tell her of my own. But I see that I exist for her as a person; she senses the exhaustion of my divorce, the demands of my children, the financial uncertainty.

We have been meeting for half a year before she talks again about aging. She is angry, confused, facing into depression. She has talked to me about so many things—being beaten as a child, leaving home at fifteen and doing domestic work, being thrown out of college as a lesbian, wandering rootlessly with no buffer between herself and male violence, working behind soda fountains and in laundries, finally finishing college and a social work degree, and finding the lover with whom she lived for fourteen years.

All that I can understand; it enriches and enlivens me even in its pain. It is the story of a survivor. It is a story that carries messages for all women.

But aging is different. I have had what I believed were strong friendships with women in their sixties, seventies, and eighties. But since they had not talked to me about aging, I assumed they had "transcended" it. Their silence on the subject made it seem unimportant, and took away the shame, fear, and guilt. I could have the illusion of the richness of difference without having to confront the reality of difference.

It does not occur to me, in 1974, that such an illusion is itself ageist—the shortcut of "we are all women together," without wanting to hear out the pain of all that has divided us. Today, in 1983, I am not ashamed of that shortcut. It came out of ignorance, but also out of knowledge. It allowed me and other women to make a leap across the forces that throughout history have aligned women with men against other women, set daughter against mother, woman of color against white woman, "lady" against servant, Arab woman against Jew, Puerto Rican woman against Black, prostitute against housewife. We are indeed all women together—our hard work unpaid and unvalued; our thoughts silenced; subject everywhere to rape and battering; in poverty, poorer; in refugee camps, the last to eat. But it should have been obvious to me, even then, that we would need to redefine the path to unity: it would demand hard traveling through a maze of barriers erected to divide us. There can be no simple act of transcendence above those barriers.

But if, in 1974, I believe in transcending race, religion, culture in my feminist analysis, at least I have spent many years in the Civil Rights struggle, and I am a Jew. I do not want to pretend that racism or Jew-hating do not exist as crimes against humanity, as principal crimes of patriarchy.

"Ageism," however, is hardly a word in my vocabulary. It has something to do with job discrimination in middle age. And aging itself I see as simply "failing," a painful series of losses, an inevitable confrontation with the human condition. Since ending patriarchy will not change the course of physical deterioration and death, we had best spend our energies on what can and desperately needs to be changed. The special problems of the aging woman—about which I have given little thought—are, I assume, only the accumulation of the problems of younger women throughout our lives. If we change the world for younger women, we change whatever can be changed for older women.

I do not know in 1974 what I know now, that old women everywhere in the world are the poorest of the poor, and in the United States are the single largest poverty group. Or that seven out of ten old people, and two-thirds of the people in our scandalous nursing "homes," are women. Or that the population of the world is undergoing explosive change, so that every day more and more old women confront the world's indifference to them. Or that aging is our "failure" and our fear because it has been so defined.

I do not know that Barbara, in her depression, is turning her face towards what is painful as a source of self-knowledge and creativity, and that my attempts to cheer or divert her are telling her to block off that source.

Nor, at 41, do I believe, really believe, that I will ever grow old.

The class is over. So is my divorce. Barbara and I continue to meet, and we become lovers. Before we do, I have a dream: she appears at my bedside looking vulnerable, older, her eyes make a silent appeal. She is no longer the woman whom, more and more, I want to spend my hours with. I feel her intolerable neediness. I am filled with pain and wake up calling out, "I can't!" to the empty bedroom.

A few weeks later, by the fireside, I ask her to stay the night. We want to spend our lives together. I set about telling my friends that I am a lesbian and, at the same time, that I love a 63-year-old woman. The questions, stated or implied: Am I looking for a mother? Is she looking for some security in her old age? Is lesbian love, then, really asexual?

But at first the difference in our ages means little to either of us. Neither Barbara nor I see her as Old, and it is inconceivable to us that others might. Only, her age sharpens my knowledge that a lifetime together is shorter than if we were in our twenties; the time together is richer for that.

Barbara begins to voice, for the first time, uneasiness about how she sees herself perceived by new friends, women in their twenties and early thirties. It is I who receive the eye contact; questions are less often addressed to her. When we go to a hardware store and Barbara asks about something, the man behind the counter looks at me when he responds. These are new experiences in Barbara's life. I have forgotten the dream in which I saw her only as Old Woman, whom I must not engage with because I could never meet her needs. Gently, lovingly, I try to persuade her that what is happening is not happening, or has other explanations. She has, after all, moved to a new community. I am unaware, of course, that it is often a move that triggers for the old woman the realization that she will no longer be seen as an ongoing person, but will be dismissed and avoided as Old.

About that time, Barbara is writing "Do You Remember Me?" and then "Look Me in the Eye." Slowly, I begin to see that the fear of the stigma of age, and total ignorance of its reality in the lives of old women, flow deep in myself, in other women I know, in the women's movement. That our society breeds ignorance and fear of both aging and death. That the old woman carries the burden of that stigma, and with remarkable, unrecognized, unrecorded courage. I begin to see that I myself am aging, was always aging, and that only powerful forces could have kept me from confronting so obvious a fact, or kept me—from self-interest alone—from working to change the social and economic realities of older women. That ageism is part of the air both Barbara and I have breathed since we were born, and that it is unthinkable that women should continue to be indifferent to the meaning of the whole of our lives, until we are old ourselves.

In "Aging, Ageism, and Feminist Avoidance," I comment that old women have struggled and still struggle "without a history, without a literature, without a politic." The process of discovery that Barbara charts in her essays, from 1977 when she began "Do You Remember Me?" to the present—claiming herself as an aging woman and confronting ageism as what it is—took place with almost nothing to turn to for confirmation. We both hope that this book will speed that process for women of all ages.

Do You Remember Me?

Barbara

I am less than five feet high and, except that I may have shrunk a quarter of an inch or so in the past few years, I have viewed the world from this height for sixty-five years. I have taken up some space in the world; I weigh about a hundred and forty pounds and my body is what my mother used to call dumpy. My mother didn't like her body and so, of course, didn't like mine. "Dumpy" was her word and just as I have had to keep the body, somehow I have had to keep the word—thirty-eight inch bust, no neck, no waistline, fat hips—that's dumpy.

My hair is grey, white at the temples, with only a little of the red cast of earlier years showing through. My face is wrinkled and deeply lined. Straight lines have formed on the upper lip as though I had spent many years with my mouth pursed. This has always puzzled me and I wonder what years those were and why I can't remember them. My face has deep lines that extend from each side of the nose down the face past the corners of my mouth. My forehead is wide, and the lines across my forehead and between my eyes are there to testify that I was often puzzled and bewildered for long periods of time about what was taking place in my life. My cheekbones are high and become more noticeably so as my face is drawn further and further down. My chin is small for such a large head and below the chin the skin hangs in a loose vertical fold from my chin all the way down my neck, where it meets a horizontal scar. The surgeon who made the scar said that the joints of my neck were worn out from looking up so many years. For all kinds of reasons, I seldom look up to anyone or anything anymore.

My eyes are blue and my gaze is usually steady and direct. But I look away when I am struggling with some nameless shame, trying to disclaim parts of myself. My voice is low and my speech sometimes clipped and rapid if I am uncomfortable; otherwise, I have a pleasant voice. I like the sound of it from in here where I am. When I was younger, some people, lovers mostly, enjoyed my singing, but I no longer have the same control of my voice and sing only occasionally now when I am alone.

My hands are large and the backs of my hands begin to show the brown spots of aging. Sometimes lately, holding my arms up reading in bed or lying with my arms clasped around my lover's neck, I see my arm with the skin hanging loosely from my forearm and cannot believe that it is really my own. It seems disconnected from me; it is someone else's, it is the arm of an old woman. It is the arm of such old women as I myself have seen, sitting on benches in the sun with their hands folded in their laps; old women I have turned away from. I wonder now, how and when these arms I see came to be my own—arms I cannot turn away from.

I live in Cambridge now in an apartment in an old Victorian kind of house with a woman I love. Above us are two men, one studying law and the other political science; and above them lives a single woman whose lover comes and stays for a few days and then he leaves to return again in a few weeks. The men who live above us are uncomfortable when they meet me in the hall, greet me without looking at me and are always in flight when we meet. The woman on the top floor does not engage with me in any way but visits with the students just below her. I wonder sometimes whether it is my lesbianism they cannot deal with or whether it is my age they cannot deal with. Usually, I conclude they do not deal with people who cannot give them something—and there is nothing I would give them in any way to aid their survival. The law student will soon be endorsing laws that will limit even further my power in the world, and the political science instructor can do me nothing but harm. The woman who lives above the men has dinner with them occasionally, and waits to see what power she can align herself with in any tenant dispute.

In the world beyond the house where we live are students riding bicycles and walking along the brick streets or lying on the grass on the Common in summer. As we walk along the avenue, we hear the conversations of the young women telling each other about Him. The pubs along the avenue are filled with the young men the girls are talking about and are building their plans for their future around. But the young men in the pubs are together, without the women, laughing loudly, taking up a great deal of space, and being served by young women anxious to please.

In contrast to the young walking through the streets, there are a few old people, moving slowly, bent over. They are mostly women, alone, carrying home a few groceries in a sack. There are a few old men. The old women do not enter the pubs; they do not drink beer, nor do they spend their evenings talking and laughing, and no young girls are waiting on them anxious to please.

But if you leave Harvard Square and walk down Cambridge Street to Inman Square—there you will find the beginnings of a small women's community. There is New Words, a bookstore of women's literature on feminism, lesbianism, the history of women. Almost any book at random confirms some of who I am and who I once was. But it is seldom that a woman past fifty ever enters the place; whenever I go I am the oldest woman there.

And if you walk on beyond New Words, you come to Bread and Roses, a women's restaurant, where the women who cook for you and serve you confirm your right to be in the world as a woman, as much as do the posters on the wall, posters of Virginia Woolf, Mary Wollstonecraft, Gertrude Stein, Emma Goldman. The food is good; and although groups of women sit together explaining, talking, laughing, there is not the struggle for space and the struggle to be heard that there is in the pubs along our avenue. And if you stay after supper on a Sunday, there may be a reading by some woman writer, or a film on Gertrude Stein or Georgia O'Keefe, or perhaps a film of Lillian Hellman's will be shown. But though all this is there to confirm the lives of women, still there is no woman there my age. I enter the restaurant and the film room always aware that I am the oldest woman there. I am glad the women's community has a beginning and is there to support women but I am aware that it is not there to confirm who *I* am. The younger women there have no place in their heads to fit me into, have no idea what I come for as no other woman my age comes, yet I am nearer the age of most of the women on their posters from whom they draw their support.

Sometimes I feel the young women are supported by other young women on the basis of a promise or a hope of who they may become, but that they demand that I somehow have already proved my right to be taken in. Sometimes I feel like the only way I'll really get into Bread and Roses—alive in the eyes of the young women—is dead, on a poster.

Wherever we go, Cynthia and I, to the pubs, to the theatre to see "The Word is Out," to hear Adrienne Rich or Olga Broumas, Mary Daly, Kate Millett, or to some meeting of the lesbian caucus of NOW, I am always the oldest woman.

I keep wondering where everybody else is. Where are the friends I drank beer with in the fifties? Where are the young women I slept with in the thirties and forties? Did they never grow old? Did they never reach sixty-five along with me? Sometimes, alone on the streets, I look about me and feel there has been some kind of catastrophe from which only I have been spared. Sometimes in desperation I search out some woman my own age on the street, or at some bus stop, or in some laundromat, to ask her, "Do you remember me? Did we drink beer together in the pubs in Seattle? Did we sleep together, you and I, in the thirties when there were no jobs and never enough to eat and love carried the whole burden to see us through?" But there is no look of recognition in her eyes. I see instead fear, I see that she is paralyzed with fear, that she does not know where my friends and lovers have gone, that she cannot remember who it was she used to be. She wants to show me pictures of her grandchildren as though all of her answers could be found there—among the living. And I go on down the street and I know there has been a catastrophe, a holocaust of my generation of women, and I have somehow been spared.

My feeling of having been spared is confirmed in the way that no one seems to be expecting me anywhere. Even if I go into a local shop to buy clothes, I am always greeted with the question, "Is this for yourself?" as though I must be buying for someone else, as though I didn't buy clothes for myself; as though I must have some supply somewhere in an old trunk, left me by my mother, there waiting for me to wear when I reached the right age.

But I have grown to like living in Cambridge. I like the sharp lines of the reality of my life here. The truth is I like growing old. Oh, it isn't that I don't feel at moments the sharp irrevocable knowledge that I have finally grown old. That is evident every time I stand in front of the bathroom mirror and brush my teeth. I may begin as I often do, wondering if those teeth that are so much a part of myself, teeth I've clenched in anger all my life, felt with my own tongue with a feeling of possession, as a cat licks her paw lovingly just because it is hers—wondering, will these teeth always be mine? Will they stay with me loyally and die with me, or will they desert me before the Time comes? But I grow dreamy brushing my teeth and find myself, unaware, planning—as I always have when I brush my teeth—that single-handed crossing I plan to make. From East to West, a last stop in the Canaries and then the trade winds. What will be the best time of year? What boat? How much sail? I go over again the list of supplies, uninterrupted until some morning twinge in my left shoulder reminds me with uncompromising regret that I will never make that single-handed crossing—probably. That I have waited too long. That there is no turning back.

But I always say probably. Probably I'll never make that single-handed crossing. Probably, I've waited too long. Probably, I can't turn back now. But I leave room now, at sixty-five, for the unexpected. That was not always true of me. I used to feel I was in a kind of linear race with life and time. There were no probably's, it was a now or never time of my life. There were landmarks placed by other generations, and I had to arrive on time or fail in the whole race.

If I didn't pass—if the sixth grade went on to the seventh without me, I would be one year behind for the rest of my life. If I graduated from high school in 1928, I had to graduate from college in 1932. When I didn't graduate from college until 1951, it took me another twenty years to realize the preceding twenty years weren't lost. But now I begin to see that I may get to have the whole thing, and that no experience longed for is really going to be missed.

"I like growing old." I say it to myself with surprise. I had not thought that it could be like this. There are days of excitement when I feel almost a kind of high with the changes taking place in my body, even though I know the inevitable course my body is taking will lead to debilitation and death. I say to myself frequently in wonder, "This is my body doing this thing." I cannot stop it, I don't even know what it is doing, I wouldn't know how to direct it. My own body is going through a process that only my body knows about. I never grew old before; never died before. I don't really know how it's done. I wouldn't know where to begin, and God knows, I certainly wouldn't know when to begin—for no time would be right. And then I realize, lesbian or straight, I belong to all the women who carried my cells for generations and my body remembers how for each generation this matter of ending is done.

Cynthia tells me now about being a young girl, watching and enjoying what her body was doing in preparation for her life. Seeing her breasts develop, watching the cleft disappear behind a cushion of dark pubic hair, discovering her own body making a bright red stain, feeling herself and seeing herself in the process of becoming.

When I was young, I watched this process with dread, seeing my breasts grow larger and larger and my hips widen. I was never able to say, "This is my body doing this wonderful unknown thing." I felt fear with every visible change, I felt more exposed, more vulnerable to attack. My swelling breasts, my widening hips, my growing pubic hair and finally the visible bleeding wound, all were acts of violence against my person, and could only bring me further acts of violence. I never knew in all the years of living in my woman's body that other women had found any pleasure in that early body experience, until Cynthia told me. But now, after a lifetime of living, my body has taken over again. I have this second chance to feel my body living out its own plan, to watch it daily change in the direction of its destiny.

When autumn comes to Cambridge, we walk arm in arm along the brick streets between Massachusetts Avenue and Concord Avenue, and I think a lot about endings because all about us endings are so visible. Dry leaves cover the brick streets, and the bare branches above us reveal now the peeling paint on the old Victorian houses and the chalky crumbling of old chimneys and brick walls. I feel how the houses are ending a period and the trees are ending a season. And in contrast to Cynthia's lighter step, her narrow waist, I become sharply aware that I, too, am living my ending.

As we walk along, other things are revealed—signs. In Cambridge, the signs are everywhere, on tree trunks, telephone poles, fences—paper signs, sometimes printed, sometimes mimeographed, hanging by the last tack or torn piece of tape. By the end of winter they will be hanging in shreds.

Someone has a need and puts their sign up. Exclamation marks remain to attest to how great the need was at the time: Garage Sale! Lost Dog! Apartment Needed! or Apartment Mate Needed! Everybody puts them up but the person with the need never comes to take the sign down. I think, as we walk along, of the experience missed—half lived—left in tatters in the wind.

Somebody decided to have a garage sale, to "get rid of things." At the end of the sale, no one came to take the sign down, to feel, "The sale is over. These things I got rid of, these things I did not."

Or in fear and pain another person pleads to every passerby to help her find her dog. But the ending is not felt; she has never removed the sign to say, "My search is over. I have found her," or "The search is over, but my dog may never return. I must become a person whose dog cannot be found."

Once someone needed an apartment, a roof, a home. She must have found one, somewhere, yet she continues to call out that she is homeless. I feel that she probably is homeless, not ever having finished with the homeless feeling—never having come back to the feeling or the place to take the sign down, to say, "It isn't the apartment I dreamed of; I wanted a garden space on a first floor—but it is my apartment now. I am the woman who now has an apartment."

And the one who wanted an apartment mate? Did she find one? Did she not find one? Does she really know whether she found one or not? She missed the ending of the experience of her need, missed the chance to say, "I will take the sign down. I will live alone. I will be the person who lives alone for awhile." Or "I will take the sign down. I have found someone who chose to live with me. I am known as the person who lives with someone."

As we walk along I see my own signs, left hanging in my life. One by one I take them down. I wanted a different body when I was young. I have lived in this body for sixty-five years. "It is a good body, it is mine."

I wanted another mother and another beginning when I was young. I wanted a mother who liked herself, who liked her body and so would like mine. "My mother did not like herself and she did not like me; that is part of the definition of who she was and of who I am. She was my mother."

When I was fifty-two, my lover left me after fourteen years of living our lives together. I wanted her to return. I waited for many years and she did not come back. "I am the woman whose lover did not return."

I was lonely for years of my life and I wandered in search of a lover. "I am a person who loves again. I am a woman come home."

So often we think we know how an experience is going to end so we don't risk the pain of seeing it through to the end. We think we know the outcome so we think there is no need to experience it, as though to anticipate an ending were the same as living the ending out. We drop the old and take up the new: drop an idea and take up a new one; drop the middle-aged and old and start concentrating on the young—always thinking somehow it's going to turn out better with a new start. I have never had a child, but sometimes I see a young woman beginning to feel the urge to have a child at about the same time she feels some disappointment at how her own life is turning out. And soon the young mother feels further disappointment when her own mother withdraws her loving investment in her daughter to pour it into her grandchild. I see how all are devalued: the grandmother devalued by society, devalued by her own self, the daughter devalued by her mother, and the granddaughter, valued not for who she is but for who she may become, racing for the landmarks, as I once did.

We never really know the beginning or the middle, until we have lived out an ending and lived on beyond it.

Of course, this time, for me, I am not going to live beyond this ending. The strangeness of that idea comes to me at the most unexpected moments and always with surprise and shock; sometimes, I am immobilized by it. Standing before the mirror in the morning, I feel that my scalp is tight. I see that the skin hangs beneath my jaw, beneath my arm; my breasts are pulled low against my body; loose skin hangs from my hips, and below my stomach a new horizontal crease is forming over which the skin will hang like the hem of a skirt turned under. A hem not to be "let down," as once my skirts were, because I was "shooting up," but a widening hem to "take up" on an old garment that has been stretched. Then I see that my body is being drawn into the earth—muscle, tendon, tissue and skin is being drawn down by the earth's pull back to the loam. She is pulling me back to herself; she is taking back what is hers.

Cynthia loves bulbs. She digs around in the earth every fall, looking for the rich loamy mold of decayed leaves and vegetation, and sometimes as she takes a sack of bone meal and works it into the damp earth, I think, "Why not mine? Why not?"

I think a lot about being drawn into the earth. I have the knowledge that one day I will fall and the earth will take back what is hers. I have no choice, yet I choose it. Maybe I won't buy that boat and that list of supplies; maybe I will. Maybe I will be able to write about my life; maybe I won't. But uncertainty will not always be there, for this is like no other experience I have ever had—I can count on it. I've never had anything before that I could really count on. My life has been filled with uncertainties, some were not of my making and many were: promises I made myself I did not keep; promises I made others I did not keep; hopes I could not fulfill; shame carried like a weight heavier each year, at my failure, at my lack of clear purpose. But this time I can rely on myself, for life will keep her promise to me. I can trust her. She isn't going to confuse me with a multitude of other choices and beckon me down other roads with vague promises. She will give me finally only one choice, one road, one sense of possibility. And in exchange for the multitude of choices she no longer offers, she gives me, at last, certainty. Nor do I have to worry this time that I will fail myself, fail to pull it off. This time, for sure I am going to make that single-handed crossing.

–1978

Look Me in the Eye

Barbara

Cynthia and I decided to go on the March to Take Back the Night. It wasn't a decision we came to easily. The notice hung on the refrigerator door for weeks. Cynthia mentioned it from time to time, and I had a vague feeling of dragging my feet, of never really saying I wanted to go but never saying I didn't. So when the evening came and we were having dinner, I knew that I had better decide how I did feel about marching or I was going to have to get up from the table, put on my coat, and go with her.

Finally, I said I didn't think the March was the right method to use for what women wanted to accomplish. "I agree with Melanie Kaye," I said. "Men don't take us seriously because they don't have to. Men don't take us seriously because they aren't physically afraid of us. Men rape women because they can."

"But Barbara, the only way to draw attention to what is happening is for women, by the thousands, to get out there in the streets and shout to the world, 'We won't put up with this violence any longer.'"

"How will shouting that you won't put up with it any longer change anything? I agree with Kaye. Men rape because they can. To go out into the streets to say that we are being raped and murdered—what does that accomplish?" For the first time it occurred to me to ask myself and to put the question to Cynthia: "What is the purpose of the March? What do we hope the March will do?"

Cynthia reached for *Equal Times* and read me her answer. "Because the night is our time of greatest fear, a time when many women are confined to their homes for fear of attack on the street, we march at night to say together, we will fight our fear, we will take back the night."

"But Cynthia, aren't the women just bluffing? What do we mean fight our fear? A woman has to be out of her mind or plain stupid not to be scared to death on the street at night. And what do we mean 'take back the night'? We're in no position to take back anything. You can't demand without power. I suspect the March is based on some hope that society doesn't really know the facts about violence against women. And that when society has the facts, it will correct the wrong. You know they won't. The facts are evident all around us. Everybody knows that women are not safe because of men's violence, and telling them again won't change anything. More than that, I think that to march through the streets saying that you are being murdered and raped and that you aren't safe except on one night in the year with several thousand women to protect you is to invite more violence. Since we have no power—all the marchers are really doing is pleading for mercy."

I always try to win an argument by throwing in a lot of words and flailing my arms around, but Cynthia didn't raise her fork or her voice. "Barbara, everything women do invites violence. We can't let others go out and not stand with them, and we need numbers, especially because it's going to rain tonight. Besides, you need the exercise."

Cynthia's last thrust was to remind me that neither of us had really walked since we got back from the summer. I agreed I needed the exercise, so we put on our rain gear and headed for the subway.

By the time we arrived at Kenmore Square I was into the spirit of the thing, and as we lined up, six in a row, I recalled some of Cynthia's earlier arguments for coming. "Maybe just because it's good for the women who are there is reason enough for going, even if it doesn't accomplish anything else," and I found myself silently agreeing that it was reason enough.

Women were dressed in somber colors, parkas, capes and slickers because of the rain. Kenmore Square was dark except for a few lights from the closed shops reflected on Commonwealth Avenue's dark wet pavement. We were lined up along the edge of the center green so as not to block traffic while we waited for the march to begin.

Monitors carrying flashlights, dressed in bright yellow slickers and hoods, moved like monks down dark corridors, back and forth along the lines, giving instructions, advising us about how long the wait would be, reminding us to watch out for the curb when we stepped into the street as we would be marching in close ranks and unable to see the curb ahead. One of the marshals, who had been assigned to our ranks and who was to march with us throughout, blew her whistle to give us our instructions: to keep our ranks closed; if a man tried to enter our ranks, to say nothing, but to join arms and partition him out to the side so that he could not enter. She cautioned us, "Try not to touch the men because that incites them."

So we are six abreast, Cynthia on the outside, and we are waiting to start when it occurs to me that there just might be a rough encounter. I don't know why I did it, maybe some of the old dyke left over in me from the '30s, but anyway, I thought having lived twenty years longer I had probably seen a lot more fracases than Cynthia had, so as we milled around in the dark impatiently waiting, I moved over to the outside. Cynthia was unaware for a few moments, then realized the switch, laughed and took her place back.

Then a man walked by with leaflets telling us that the real oppressor was not men but capitalism, and I was about to ask him what the hell he thought the difference was when I remembered our instructions. Feeling like a race horse waiting at the gate, I snort, stamp my feet and wait.

I felt the exhilaration, the oneness with the women around me, the sense of at last doing something instead of passively grinding my teeth with anger, as I do every morning when I pick up the *Globe* to see what woman was murdered the night before. I felt the energy of the Wanderground, the conviction that the war was real and the Day would come.

I don't know exactly when I sensed that something was wrong and noticed that Cynthia was no longer beside me but a few feet away where the monitor was talking to her. I joined them. At first the conversation was not clear to me and I glanced at Cynthia's face for some clue. There was none. The monitor was at first evasive and then chose her words with care, "If you think you can't keep up, you should go to the head of the march." Gradually, I took in, like a series of blows, what the situation was, that the monitor had thought that, because my hair is grey, because I am sixty-five and because I look sixty-five, I might be unable to keep up; that her concern was that I might, if slower, leave a gap between the ranks in which men might try to enter; and that she could not say this to me. I stepped directly in front of the monitor for eye to eye contact to force her to talk to me instead of about me, saying only to Cynthia, "She means me, Cynthia."

I faced the monitor with rage. "You have got to be kidding; I don't believe this." My fists were clenched at the injustice as I felt the all too familiar wave of helplessness and fury engulf me. Then, in the glow of the flashlight, I saw the monitor's face and heard her words of discomfort and confusion. She said that she was sorry, that she had not known what to do, whether to say anything to me or not, and finally she had asked others if she should. She wanted to apologize. I said it was all right but it wasn't all right. Sometimes I wonder if it will ever be all right.

She went back to her monitoring and I tried to go back to where I had been in my head before the encounter. Back to the exhilaration, back when I was feeling and remembering Cynthia's words, "if the march doesn't accomplish anything else, it is good for the women doing it." But there was no way back. I took my place beside Cynthia but I knew that this march could not be good for me. The monitor came back to me a second time; she wanted to apologize again, she explained that she had not known what to do. I assured her I understood that she had not known what to do. For at that moment, I did not know, myself, what I thought she should have done.

We continued to wait in the darkness but nothing was the same. I felt the old caution I used to feel entering a bar not knowing whether or not it was a men's only bar—the dread of being told I did not belong there. With the same furtiveness, I now glanced at the women around me, at the six women in the rank ahead of me. We had been laughing together earlier at the man who wanted to convince us that capitalism was our oppressor; at least, I had thought we were laughing together—now I wondered. I looked at the women in the row behind me. I wondered how I looked to them. My short stature, my grey hair, my wrinkled face—I wondered how sixty-five years looked to them. And finally I looked at the four other women who were to walk beside me. I wondered how they felt about being with me. I wondered if I should take the arm of the woman next to me and tried to remember the instructions, but all I could recall was my shock and shame, hearing the monitor's words, "If you can't keep up, go to the head of the march." Hearing once more that I was a problem and did not fit. All my life in a man's world, I was a problem because I was a woman; now I'm a problem in a woman's world because I'm a sixty-five year old woman. Hearing once more that I was not in the right place and thinking, "If not here, where?"

Finally, we heard the signal to start and with hesitancy I took the arm of the woman next to me. I wondered if she had some idea that I needed her support. God knows I needed hers and everybody else's, but not for walking; my rage alone would have carried me twenty miles and a foot off the pavement.

The march was a strange scene from where I was. We passed through blocks of dark apartment houses where only scattered lights indicated anyone was home. It felt more like marching through an empty city in which only a few people were left. In front of many of the apartment buildings, four or five men stood outside together; women could be seen at the windows above, some waving, some not.

I chanted with the rest:

We have the power
We have the right
The streets are ours
And we'll prove it tonight.

But I heard the lie in my own voice.

We are angry, proud and strong
Freedom is our righteous song.

I studied the wet pavement under my feet and tried to get some hold on what had happened. I wondered how to feel proud and strong when women around me were telling me I was weak. I wondered how I looked to other people and I kept feeling my own muscles and reassuring myself, "Barbara, you don't feel very weak to me." I wondered what Cynthia was feeling and I wondered if I would ever have the confidence to make love to her again.

At one point, hating myself and the women around me, I found myself wishing some of the grinning men on the curb would start something so I could put my fist in somebody's face. I shouted:

Puerto Rican, Black and White
Same struggle, same fight

and I wondered where I came in. I was tired of young women who could not look me in the eye, of the monitor who could talk about me but not to me. I was tired and distrustful of a women's movement that seemed to feel everyone's oppression but mine and I wondered why in hell I was there.

Sometimes as we were marching, I would look at some woman leaning out of her apartment window and I would think, "Why don't you get some guts and come on out and join us?" But then I would think, "Don't come out if you're over sixty, the greeting you get will send you right back in again."

We finished the march and hung around Blackstone Park for awhile. Some woman with a tape recorder for New England Today, a radio program, stopped and asked if Cynthia and I would comment on the march. I said that I wished more women had come out of their houses but in the back of my mind I was wondering, "Why did this woman ask me? Does she want the Older Woman's Viewpoint?"

Finally, we took the subway home.

But I was left with the experience—with the rage that had no place to go. I could see no way to put the anger on the monitor and I fought not to put it on my aging body. I recalled the monitor's face above her flashlight, sincere in her discomfort and apology—that she "had not known what to do." I tried to look at it from where she was. What could she do? The ranks were expected to stay close together in order that men could not enter. There might be a lot of women who could not keep up. And how could she know whether they could or not without asking? And why should I find her assumption that I might not be able to keep up so painful?

Repeatedly, I told myself that there would be nothing wrong with being physically weak. Lots of people are. If it does not happen to be true of me now, it will be true of me soon. If I have pride in my strength now, it is false pride and if I feel shame in my lack of strength later, I will have let someone else in my head for the rest of my life.

I would go over it all again in my mind. The monitors were looking for women who would march slower, I told myself, and I looked sixty-five and they picked me. But why me? Out of five thousand women there must have been thirty about to come down with the flu, fifty suffering from a hang-over, and at least a hundred who were going to get a blister on their heel before the march was over. So why me? If you are a woman about to come down with the flu or your head is bursting with a hang-over you will either decide not to march or have sense enough to quit. Why can't it also be assumed that if a sixty-five-year-old woman doesn't feel up to a march, she won't choose to march? I still come to only one conclusion: the monitor didn't pick me out because I looked weak; she picked me out because she believes that a sixty-five-year-old woman lacks judgment about what she can do. She thought I did not perceive the situation and that I did not know what I was doing.

We had chanted:

Our bodies, our lives
Our right to decide.

Did she think I had no right to decide?

Sixty-five is older—that's true. Sixty-five may be slower—that's also true. But who should know more about what sixty-five can do than the woman who is living it? All our lives, we look over a situation and decide whether or not to participate according to our ability. From six to ninety-six, we measure our strength and our agility for the situation at hand. Why did the monitor assume that I had suddenly lost that ability at sixty-five?

One may reply to this that it is well known that very old people lack judgment. I'm not willing to accept even that general statement. Lots of people lack judgment—drunk people, psychotic people, plain happy excited people. But old and lacking judgment don't go together—old and cautious sometimes do. When I was young, it seemed like everybody over thirty thought, "The young lack judgment." Now I'm sixty-five, and the women in their thirties think I lack judgment, and I am not about to go through that round for a second time without examining very carefully this movement that is rejecting me.

As I thought about it, I could see that the women's movement, the second wave, has just come of age; she is barely twenty-one. She is made up largely of young women in their twenties and thirties who are concerned with their physical strength as well as their political strength. And well they should be. For the generations of women who came before them were considered by men to be weak (despite considerable evidence to the contrary), and women, as a result, viewed themselves as weak, thus limiting the development of their bodies even more. Physical weakness, all too soon, was equated with being mentally inferior and women were segregated out of the mainstream of power, put on a pedestal or at the head of the line, where the "weaker sex" was in even a greater position of vulnerability.

But the young women who make up the movement today are physically stronger and want to feel their physical strength. They are jogging, running in marathons, working out in gyms to build up muscle, practicing karate and judo. And, it seems, the young women are beginning to worry about what to do with other women they consider "weak." Again, the equation is quickly made that physically weaker, is mentally weaker and the next thought is to separate them out. (Put them at the front of the line.)

I could see that, in another setting, I might not have felt the humiliation and, later, the fear so acutely. But this march was a march to say, "We are strong and we will not be victimized by men." So the message of the younger woman, "You are older and weak," I could only hear as "You make us vulnerable by your weakness. You are the weak link in our strong chain, so go to the front of the line."

Later, as I began to internalize the message and to hear it from within instead of from without, my fear grew. I saw that I lived in an unsafe world as all women do. Male violence is everywhere. But at a time when young women are building up physical strength to combat the violence, I am growing older and will be growing weaker. On a dark street, hearing footsteps behind me, I will be less able to run, less able to ward off a weapon or a fist, and less able to call out and be heard. My fear of such a scene paralyzed me.

Alone, I examined my predicament. As I took in the inevitability of my becoming less and less able to protect myself, all I could feel was a kind of hopelessness and panic. But then I did what I have always done in my life when I had to face some given, some painful reality that cannot be changed, that will not go away, that must be lived with in some way. I thought, "Then I will yield to this fear. If it is something that must be, then it must be and I will not fight what I know I cannot win with."

But as the panic began to subside, it dawned on me that men have always been stronger than I was. This was no new experience that was going to come with aging. Men were stronger than I was when I was in my twenties and in my thirties and in my forties, and it would never have occurred to me in those years to give up without a fight. I realized that my feelings of shame grew out of the fear that I would not fight—that I would betray myself. In place of the fear came old primitive knowledge, animal knowledge. The knowledge of the animal who lives her life out; who, blind with age, will smell and feel her way to the end of life. Who, old and blind, with her back to the wall, will face the enemy, bare her teeth and inflict whatever wound she can on animal or man, twice her size, who thinks he has come upon some easy prey. As long as she has strength left, she will not feed the enemy; not one more meal from her flesh will she give to strengthen him.

Thus I healed myself and could feel whole again, connected to my aging body, wanting to live my life out in partnership with it, without feelings of humiliation because of its difference, and without the fear that I would so want to disclaim it that I would fail to protect it.

Although much of what happened to me in the march is resolved for me, I am still angry at the ageism in the women's movement. I am angry at what it does to me and at what it must be doing to many other women of my age. It also makes me distrustful of the movement itself, as it seems to me that such ageism, entrenched in the minds of the women of this second wave, must be some indication of the degree to which we have all internalized male values.

And then I began to wonder: Where are the Susan B. Anthonys, the Carrie Nations, the Pankhursts today? These post-menopausal women were marching all over the place a hundred years ago, and no one was asking them if they could keep up. It was then I realized that this is probably the first time in history that the mass of rebelling angry women are so young. In the first wave in this country and in England, angry women in mid-life and older were marching and visible. In the photographs in Emmeline Pankhurst's *My Own Story,* I see older women marching with younger women, and older women were smashing windows and setting fires all over London, and women in mid-life and older were going to prison and going on hunger strikes and being force fed.

Emmeline Pankhurst, herself, was fifty-nine when she marched to King's Gate and was arrested. She also describes the very old women who accompanied her when she was fifty-three and the deputation marched with their petition to the Prime Minister:

> Then our deputation set forth. Accompanying me as leader were two highly respectable women of advanced years, Mrs. Saul Solomon, whose husband had been the Prime Minister of the Cape, and Miss Neligan, one of the foremost of the pioneer educators of England. We three and five other women were preceded by Miss Elaine Howey, who, riding fast went on horseback to announce our coming.

Thus I suspect it would have been unheard of in the first wave to stop an older woman in a march and question her about whether she could keep up.

It is probably evidence of our growth and increasing strength that for the first time younger women make up the mass of the second wave. Made possible for the first time because young women are more knowledgeable than they were a hundred years ago, better read and with more literature to read than ever before. And freer, because the younger woman of today is not caught in enforced heterosexual coupling until much later in her life and may, in fact, not choose heterosexuality. A hundred years ago, much of the radical feminist political action was probably not visible to most young women, who were in domestic servitude or were already burdened with unwanted pregnancies and small children, unable to read and with no way out. This increased visibility of young women is certainly due, in part, to the efforts of the older women of the first wave.

But the primary reason that the second wave is made up of young women is that the second wave rose out of a different time in patriarchal history—it rose out of a time of a patriarchally supported white middle class youth culture. This important difference in the two waves is not one that I can dismiss lightly with the popular observation that emphasis on youth neglects an older population. That is to trivialize what has been taking place since the first wave and the development of the youth culture. It does not make clear to me what happened to me in the Boston march. It does not explain to me why I do not have eye to eye contact with younger women as I enter my mid sixties, and it does not explain to me what happened to the older feminist activists who were such an important part of our earlier history.

In the first wave, when the angry older women were marching, most women were slaves to their husbands; as were his children whom he could put to work in factories, mines, or into domestic servitude as soon as they were strong enough. The mother had no real power over her life and no real power over the lives of her children. But it was profitable for the father to give the mother seeming authority over the children. In his absence, she represented his authority and kept the children in subjection. Frequently she was beaten by her husband for her children's insubordination, and she in turn beat the children to keep them in line.

But with the advent of child labor laws and children's rights, the father lost power over his children. Out from under the father's tyranny, the children were a burden and an expense instead of a source of income, and they became solely the woman's problem. The mother still had the care of the children, but now she had to try to control them without the father's power. Once the father had said to the mother, "I want them fed; feed them. I want them clothed for the workplace; clothe them. I want them God-fearing and industrious; teach them. I want them obedient; beat them." But now it was not in the father's interest to control the children, and he did not transfer his power to the mother. Instead, she was left powerless to protect herself from their battering demands. The children, out from under the tyranny of the father's rule, were free in their own way to tyrannize the powerless mother. Now it was the children who borrowed power from the father, who were saying to her, "Feed me, clothe me. Buy me everything. The fathers say you must." And indeed the fathers are saying clearly, "The children must have everything. If you are a good mother, your children's laundry will be Downy soft and perfumed. You will tempt your children's appetites and feel pride to hear them demand, 'More sausages, Mom.'" You will send them out in white clothes to play in the mud to prove that you know how to wash their clothes cleaner than the woman next door. You will make sure the environment your children live in is scrubbed, polished, sanitized and odorless. You will wipe their noses and bottoms with the softest tissue in the world, all the time rubbing your hands in lotion so your callouses and red cracks won't feel rough on your children's soft skin."

It seems to me that never in such a few years has the patriarchy been able to develop a new elite leisure class of consumers and a slave class to serve them—an elite class that stays out of the job market and does not threaten the father's job, but consumes endlessly to ensure his job.

A hundred years ago, the mother's value to the Fathers was that she raised God-fearing industrious children who could bring income into the family until they left home. Now the mother's value to the Fathers is that she raises children to expect the best, to be good consumers, to remain as children as long as possible and out of the job market and she hopes that society will value her for how well she serves them. The elitism of the children is still exploitation of the children. Now, instead of the exploitation by the single father, it is the exploitation by the collective Fathers. But the woman is still slave, and now she has two masters to serve.

Today, the evidence is all around us that youth is bonded with the patriarchy in the enslavement of the older woman. There would, in fact, be no youth culture without the powerless older woman. There can be no leisure elite consuming class unless it is off the back of someone. The older woman is who the younger women are better than—who they are more powerful than and who is compelled to serve them. This is not true of men; older men still have power, power to be president, power to be Walter Cronkhite, and power to marry younger women. Men are not the servants of youth; older women are.

The lines between the powerful and the powerless have always had to be very clearly drawn, and nowhere is this more evident than in the clothes of men, the young, and women. The clothes of the young woman are designed to, at least, give the illusion of power and freedom, and the clothes of the older woman are designed to make her look sexless, dowdy, and separated from the rest of society. Little boys and young men for high occasions dress fashionably like older men, in suit and vest, but no young woman dresses fashionably by imitating the dress of older women.

It becomes more clear that the present attitude of women in their twenties and thirties has been shaped since childhood by patriarchy to view the older woman as powerless, less important than the fathers and the children, and there to serve them both; and like all who serve, the older woman soon becomes invisible.

From the back of the house to the front of the march is not that different—both result in invisibility. In a march of five thousand women, all you have to do is separate out the women in their sixties; and unless the observer happens to see the first few lines of the march, she watches five thousand women go by and is left with the impression that there is not a sixty-year-old woman among them.

I watched the 80 "Women to Watch in the '80s" go by in *Ms.* magazine last month, and I learned that there are only six women in their fifties worth watching and only one woman in her sixties worth watching. That's invisibility.

I find the whole line-up of women to watch in the '80s very patriarchal and I would prefer not to see it at all. But worse, *Ms.* magazine asked older women to make the selection, a selection that excluded them. That's one way to get permission to oppress—ask the older woman, not to be coequal, but to step aside for the younger woman. Sheila Tobias stepped aside by saying, "established women have the responsibility to boost others. One reason the first wave of feminism died out is that it failed to create new leaders."

To me something in her statement smacks of maternal self-sacrifice and invisibility: the young women asked Tobias to make herself invisible and she made herself invisible. Nor do I think that the first wave of feminism died because the women failed to create new leadership. I think it died because the women decided to put their own needs aside to help the good old boys win a war; and when they got ready to take up the struggle again, they discovered they were slave to two masters.

Given the nature of the question put to Tobias, it is not surprising that she responded in patriarchal language: the word *boost* suggests help on "the way up," someone on the bottom boosting another to a higher level. Such an image conjures up the possibility that the one being boosted may well have her foot on the booster. Such a word seems a long way from the beginnings of this second wave that consciously avoided hierarchical structure.

I hurt that the committee who selected the eighty women to watch tells me that I am invisible, that no sixty-five-year-old woman is still in process and worth watching; but they give no better message to the women who are pictured there in their forties, as it must be plain to them that they will be invisible in ten years, in their fifties and sixties.

Several months have gone by since Cynthia and I went to the Boston march, and I only begin to see how I came to be there at sixty-five in this particular time in our history and how the monitor came to be there. I only begin to see who we both are and how men are still defining our feelings about ourselves and each other.

–1979

Notes

The allusion to Melanie Kaye refers to her essay "Women and Violence," *Sinister Wisdom* #9 (Spring 1979), p. 77.

The Wanderground refers to Sally M. Gearheart's novel of that name (Watertown: Persephone, 1979), which envisions a time when women have freed themselves from heterosexuality and live on their own land, protected by their own militancy.

The passage from Emmeline Pankhurst's *My Own Story* (New York: Source Book Press, 1914) is found on page 199.

Exploitation by Compassion

Barbara

I wrote this article for a women's newspaper after my return from the United Nations Conference on the Status of Women held in Copenhagen in 1980. This was the midpoint of the United Nations Decade for Women that began in 1975. The only note of optimism, after five years, was that women, who had been left out of their nations' statistics, were at last visible.

I was stunned by what was revealed. Document after document, country after country, uncovered the facts of women's exploitation—their longer working hours, their unpaid labor, their greater poverty, the higher toll of apartheid on women, the growth of multinational corporations at women's expense, the bulldozing effects of "development" that gives jobs to men and takes land from women. One U.N. representative described refugee camps as rows of thin, hungry women and children and a few well-fed men.

I came home to look at our own lines of unemployed teachers, and although their suffering was not comparable, the process by which they got in those lines was not that different from what was taking place worldwide.

But I was also coming home from a conference where not only had I been one of the oldest women there, I had been unaware of that fact or its meanings. The issues of old women worldwide were never addressed at the conference, and I had been unaware of that also. Although I did not see that absence as clearly as I see it today, I did know that I wanted to use the Copenhagen conference in a way that would bring women of all ages together before the unpaid and low paid labor of younger women was exploited once again—this time in the name of old women—and before the two generations were pitted against each other.

Are you without a regular job—one with a regular pay check, a health plan, vacation leave, and a retirement plan? Are you working part-time, sometimes? Are you on food stamps?

Do you stand in line for your unemployment check and wonder what you will do when you get the last one? Do you keep wondering how you got there? Do you have the feeling there must be something that you aren't doing right?

Well, I just got back from the U.N. Conference of the Decade for Women, in Copenhagen, and I think there may be some answers there for all of us. They may not be answers we like and they may not be the answers the U.N. had in mind—but answers nevertheless.

First, we got in that line just by being women. And if there is anything we aren't doing right, it is that we aren't mad enough—yet. In fact, what each day of the Conference made increasingly clear to me was that women have not even begun to conceive of how mad they are going to have to get in order to get out of the lines we are standing in. And women are standing in lines all over the world.

We have been going in and out of the unemployment lines as long as I can remember and as long as my mother, or yours, can remember. And history ought to tell us that getting another job is not going to get us out.

I want to talk about looking ahead, but just for a moment let's look at those lines. During the Second World War, most of us were out of the home and into the labor force. That should have gotten us a permanent job and out of the line— but it didn't. When the war was over, we let ourselves be programed right back into the home again and into the baby business.

When the babies began to flood an unprepared public education system, we were channeled into teaching the elementary grades. We found that the woman principal we had when we were in school was not to be seen. They had named the school after her and then replaced her with a male principal, a male vice-principal, and a male superintendent or two. We could see that there was going to be no "way up" but we took the job anyway because we needed it.

But then came birth control, and now the educators have decided not to improve public education by making classes smaller. Instead, they've begun to close many elementary schools. The teachers are back in line again—that is, the women are back.

When are we going to learn that new factories, new industries, new technology, and even new services make permanent jobs, but not for women? When are we going to learn that we are being pulled in and out of the labor market for the convenience of a male world?

And what do you think society has in mind for us next? I think I know.

The Copenhagen Conference had documents on every table. The International Labor Organization, for example, put out a lot of statistics just for the occasion. These documents provided interesting information about the spot we're in:

○ "Most women are permanently working but not permanently employed." (To this we can only add, "How true.")

○ "That they constitute half the population is a demographic fact. That they perform one-third of the total work hours in the market is also making an entry into official statistics." (Any woman has to wonder why it took this long to enter these facts into the official statistics.)

○ "Beyond the market, their labor amounts to twice as many work hours as in the market. It is this huge chunk of unpaid labor that neither the market has measured nor society recognized." (Any really mad woman has to ask, "How come it took you so long?")

I came home from Copenhagen loaded with documents—documents from the ILO, the U.N. agencies, and the U.S. Bureau of Labor Statistics. They were all apologetic about having left us out all these years and about having made us invisible. They implied that things were going to be better from now on because they have the facts and a wonderful new technology for getting even more statistics. I sat on the plane coming home from Copenhagen, and I sure felt better.

Whenever I read stuff like this, I have the reassured feeling that when they get all the statistics together and the facts are in, they (whoever "they" is) are going to use them for my benefit. *They* are going to make sure I'm rewarded and they won't be expecting any more free services—*they* are going to get me out of that line.

So I got off the plane and I hurried home to read the rest of the documents and to get to the good part about what *they* plan to do for me. Well, I can tell you now (and I read them all), *there isn't any plan there.* There isn't anything to suggest that they are going to use the new data for my benefit—or yours.

So before we celebrate the new statistical visibility of women, history should suggest to us that visibility may not lessen our exploitation. It may, in fact, only increase it. If women are being moved in and out of the labor force for the convenience of a male world, it just figures that they can exploit women more efficiently if they know just how many are standing in line vulnerable and needing to work for any pay.

I'm hoping maybe this time we can get smart and see if we can figure out what the male world has in mind for us next, and whether they have in mind more invisible "free services" or whether they are about to build another male empire, like public education, and are looking for some cheap woman labor.

When I got back from Copenhagen, I thought I had a clear idea of all of woman's invisible work—her child care, her nursing, her cleaning, her cooking, her entertaining.

Then I saw a CBS documentary called, "What Are We Going to Do about Mother?" I also saw a public service announcement put out by the Franciscans. I realized that I had only seen the tip of the iceberg of woman's invisible work, her "free services."

First, the CBS documentary: Lucille Hays is 83 and she has been living for two years with her son and daughter-in-law, Jack and Marie. She has chronic heart and lung disease, and she explains from her wheelchair:

"In my generation we expected to take care of our parents. They didn't have so many hospitals and things. We always took care of grandma and grandpa until they died, no matter how poor we were, how hard it was for us, or anything. I know my parents did."

But then Marie's own parents suffer mild strokes and also come to live with the Hays'. Suddenly Marie Hays, who is about 45 and has just finished raising three children, finds herself running what amounts to a small nursing home. We see her on the phone desperately trying to find a home for her parents, but the cheapest place she can find in Pittsburgh is $49 a day. Even though her parents own their own home in Pittsburgh and have managed to save $40,000, they have to move to Florida to find a place they can afford that provides care—and that is near another daughter.

The narrator of the documentary gave some very interesting statistics: In 1900, about the time Lucille Hays' parents were taking care of her parents, there weren't as many old people and they didn't live as long. In 1900, there were only three million Americans over the age of 65; now there are twenty-four million. By the year 2030, one out of every six Americans is going to be over 65. Most of them will be women.

We, as women, had better ask ourselves what these figures mean. Old in this country means poor. And older and poorer means women. And you and I know that when Lucille Hays says that her "parents" took care of her grandparents, she means that her mother—a woman—took care of them.

Dr. Monica Blumenthal, a geriatric psychiatrist, commented on the documentary. She explained that right now there are a million Americans who require twenty-four hour care. Medicare is not picking up this burden, since it serves "acute" not "chronic" illness. It's a myth, she explained, that the aged are being cared for in institutions. The fact is that they are being cared for by their families.

"It's almost always a girl, a female child. And my impression is that the family nominates one person, saying,

'This is your job'... Interestingly enough, the family usually abandons this one person and doesn't lend a hand any more."

So the problem of the aged falls on the daughters—and the daughters-in-law. Because men frequently marry younger women, it will probably be the husband's aging parent who comes into the home first (unless he has a sister whose husband won't object to living with an in-law). And the aging parent will probably be a woman, because women live longer than men. She herself will probably have nursed an aging husband until he died, and may even have nursed and buried a second husband. Why? Because when a man is widowed, he looks for a wife to take care of him. He finds a younger widow who needs a home and whose only way to survive is to do the one thing she knows—take care of another man.

And now for the public service announcement put out by the Franciscans to raise public consciousness about the homelessness of the aging woman.

First, we see the woman in her doctor's office where she has just learned to use a walker, probably for arthritis. She is telling her doctor that she does not see how she is going to manage alone. Her doctor says, "Don't you have a daughter out West?"

Next we see her traveling across the country on a bus, worried about how she will be received in her daughter's house as a dependent old woman. Across the nation, the solution is implied, "*Don't you have a daughter?*"

The problem of the staggering increase in the numbers of aging women is about to explode on the American scene, and society has only one plan for solving it—off the backs of women.

We need to take stock of the seriousness of the situation now while there is still time (we hope!) or our lives are going to be programed for us again. Teachers are right now in the unemployment lines and right now, here in Boston, some elementary schools are being remodeled as nursing homes for the elderly. How long will it be before the teachers will be pulled out of the line again and back into the remodeled schoolhouse?

As long as society is able to have the care of the elderly done in the home as women's invisible work, you can be sure, it will. The poor will be expected to do what they have always had to do, make room for two more in an overcrowded, sub-standard dwelling that is a fire trap for the able-bodied and a funeral pyre for the aged.

There's a new hitch, though. When this problem hits the great middle class, they won't be able to solve it, as the last generation did, by adding a room, or making an apartment out of the recreation room. They are going to be crowded in condominiums and society is going to have to provide for the aged outside the home.

But in the home or out of the home, caring for the aged is still going to be women's work. We had better decide now what kind of work that is going to be.

Is it going to be a permanent job with a regular pay check, a health plan, a paid vacation leave, and a retirement plan built in? Is it going to be the kind of job that keeps you out of the unemployment line? Or are we, again, going to be what the ILO describes as "permanently working but never permanently employed"?

We had better decide now, because the male world is getting ready to build another service empire that will make the takeover of public education look like peanuts.

Think about it—one out of every six Americans over 65. You're going to walk through the Boston Common in a few years and think you're in St. Petersburg, Florida. And don't think that that aging population is going to be pushed aside. It isn't—not because of a new wave of humanitarianism but a new wave of much needed economic growth.

We, as women, may look at this new aging population and think poor and think women. But that's not what the boys are thinking.

They are already thinking of a whole new building industry, of new housing and nursing facilities. They will invent every kind of gadget ever dreamed of to help the elderly. They will design special chairs, dishes, clothes, beds. There is no end to what the male mind can come up with where there is a market and where public monies flow.

The men are already beginning to gather. Hugh Downs is the MC for the TV program for senior citizens, "Over Easy," and James Callahan is the MC for "Senior Circle," although the mass of their viewers are women.

Thomas Mahoney (recently retired from MIT) is now Secretary for Senior Affairs in Massachusetts. With a budget of $56 million he is planning four "congregate housing" facilities where thirty to forty apartments with a common dining room will house the elderly in four areas of Massachusetts. You get the picture.

Like public education, these new services will require experts of all kinds—consultants, administrators, directors, supervisors—and all male (if we don't fight it). And finally women will do the real work—cheap if they can get us.

Right now we have some leverage—leverage we didn't have when we got caught in free housework and childcare. We know what this new work is worth.

Right now it's worth $49 a day per person in Pittsburgh. But will we have the guts to hold out for that? Are we mad enough to hold out for that? Mad enough to say "no" to cheaper care and mad enough to ask our mothers to say "no" to our cheap service?

I have the feeling that we are ripe for exploitation and are ready to be ripped off once more by the male world. Generations of voices have told us that we are compassionate, caring women.

Even our own women's movement is telling us that the generation gap is an expression of ageism, and that we need to recognize what our mothers have been through. And indeed, we do need to recognize what our mothers have been through if we are to avoid repeating their life experience of invisible work.

But if we face the problem of caring for our mothers with sentimentality, the male world will rip us off for sure. Perhaps we can avoid the old compassion trap this time, and face the problem with true sentiment, caring not only what happens to our aging mothers *but also what happens to ourselves.*

What kind of care will our mothers have and what kind of job will we have? What kind of facility will they live in and what kind of place will we work in?

Will these services be administered by women? Will we have policies that protect our mothers—and someday ourselves—from male profiteering and meaningless technology?

Will we have personnel policies that assure us of a job with a regular pay check, a health plan, a paid vacation and a retirement plan—a job that keeps us out of the unemployment line?

The answer to all these questions is probably not. Certainly not if we don't get mad—mad enough to insist on some change. Mad enough to care, *really* care about our mothers and ourselves.

–1980

Aging, Ageism and Feminist Avoidance

Cynthia

This essay was written as a review of The Social World of Old Women, *by Sarah H. Matthews (Beverly Hills: Sage Publications, 1979).*

When I was standing in line to buy this book, a woman behind me, possibly in her mid-fifties, stared at the cover and asked eagerly, "Is that a good book?" And then, immediately afterwards, "It's not depressing, is it?"

So far the women's movement has resonated with its silence on the subject of the status of old women. As if our old women were indeed too depressing for us, or an embarrassment to us, or beyond the reach of our feminist analysis. Even when we have sought out an old woman for her oral history (our women's past)—for example, Kramer and Masur's interviews with Jewish old women or the Black Women's Oral History Project—we have shown notably little interest in the challenges of her life today as an aging woman (our women's future).[1] Nor has the lesbian feminist movement, which has supplied the energy and analysis for breaking down so many false barriers between women, yet begun to chip away at the wall separating young women from old. The Older Women's League was founded two years ago to change the policies that force older women into poverty, but so far their concerns have scarcely touched the women's movement as a whole. With few exceptions—usually our romanticizing of a grandmother or our fantasizing of a Wise Old Woman—our literature, our music, our visual images, our political analyses and organizing, tell us less about old women than about how thoroughly we younger women have absorbed male society's avoidance (masking a deep underlying terror and hatred) of our aging selves.

The Social World of Old Women is an important work because it records and challenges that avoidance. Certainly, Matthews' title is far too sweeping. But by directing our attention to the social world of even some old women and the issues of their lives, she provides us at least with a place to begin to examine our own attitudes. In fact, although old women far outnumber old men, and more than twice as many old women as men live in poverty, Sarah Matthews' book is (to my knowledge) the only book in existence that focuses exclusively on the lives of women over 65 and the ageism they confront.[2]

Matthews is a sociologist who volunteered for a year in a senior citizen's center. Her book is based on that experience, and on interviews with thirty-eight white widows (all of them mothers) who were living alone and who had applied, sometimes successfully, for public housing. These women were over seventy; many were over eighty. But a large number of them thought they shouldn't be interviewed because they weren't old. If that strikes you as cute, or a sign of a healthy attitude, or surprising, or stupid, it is essential for you to read this book.

What *The Social World of Old Women* illuminates best is the enormous life energy that these women expend in trying to deal with the stigma of age. Without a history, without a literature, without a politic, they find it impossible to reconcile their sense of themselves—as real women, whose lives are ongoing—with the new, degrading ways in which they find themselves seen (or rendered unseen), or with their own lifelong training in ageism.

An important strategy for preserving their personhood against all odds becomes what Matthews calls "information management." In blunter terms, the old woman tries to pass. "I don't think they know my age... People don't think I'm as old as I am, so I don't go around blabbin' it." Another old woman recommends "taking on the qualities associated with youth. People will never think about your age. They'll just think how young you are."

Passing—except as a consciously political tactic for carefully limited purposes—is one of the most serious threats to selfhood. We attempt, of course, to avoid the oppressor's hateful distortion of our identity and the real menace to our survival of his hatred. But meanwhile, our true identity, never acted out, can lose its substance, its meaning, even for ourselves. Denial to the outside world and relief at its success ("Very few people think of me as old as I am. They don't. People can't tell how old I am.") blurs into denial to self ("I'm always surprised when I look down and see all that gray hair, because I don't feel gray-headed").

Given the hazards of passing and the fact that so many old people themselves have lived a lifetime of fear, contempt, and patronizing of the old, it is easy to see why most old people "share with other members of society the stereotypical view of old people" and also refuse to define themselves as old. Matthews suggests that "flexibility in the definition (of age) is an advantage," but her book more strongly warns that "you're as young as you think you are" is a deeply self-alienating defense. To be surprised, time after time, by my own gray hair on the hairdresser's floor is to be cut off from direct knowledge of my identity, from the adventure of my growth, from nature and her day-to-day processes at work in my own being. That surprise reflects my rejection, not simply of the stigma of age, but of the reality of age. It links me with my oppressor and divides me from myself. Gray hair is ugly, age is wrong; I cannot be that ugly and wrong. I cannot be the woman with gray hair.

It also divides me from other women. "What occurs," says Matthews, "is that the old woman has one definition for other old people and one for herself." That division can compound my isolation as well as rendering me politically impotent. If I see myself as young (interesting, intelligent, pleasant looking, engaged with life) and see other women my age as old (dull, stupid, ugly, worthless), I will prefer friends younger than myself. But the younger woman sees me either as old (dull, stupid, ugly, worthless) or, as I see myself, as "exceptional." Exceptional, like passing, is a dangerous defense. It means that a single slip can trigger off "old."

Matthews examines what it is like to live with that defense, in a world where your personhood is in continual doubt. Awkward enough at any age to forget a name or a face. But when we are old, a simple error—such as we frequently made in our twenties or thirties—can consign us (in others' eyes and possibly our own) to being written off as "senile," not worth knowing. A social faux-pas becomes a disaster, and the definition of a faux-pas broadens. Matthews describes how one woman at a senior citizen's event stared at a downpour in dismay. She had brought her raincoat but then left it in the car because "I thought you'd laugh at me if I brought it in, old grandma with her raincoat and boots." To forget your raincoat is to be a forgetful old woman, to bring it with you is to be a fussy old woman. There is no way to be.

Because most younger women are rejecting or patronizing, old women often avoid their presence. A number of the women Matthews interviewed, despite their own prejudices against old age, much preferred age-segregated housing ("I mix with my own age"). But while the polite turning away of younger people in social situations is intensely painful, street encounters are more raw. There the silent messages of rejection are given a voice.

> I was walking home from shopping. I guess it was Thursday. And there was this young fella, see, and his friends. I was carrying my groceries. They were heavy. And I was walking, you know, kind of slow. And that young fella called, "Why aren't you in your grave?" He and his friend laughed.

Another woman, smiling at a group of small children as she passes, is told, "You're ugly, ugly, ugly."

In her chapter, "The Importance of Setting in the Lives of Old Widows," Matthews highlights the meaning of the displacement of old women from their neighborhoods. Urban "renewal"—condominium conversion, the gentrification of a neighborhood—is usually seen as a hardship for the old woman not only for the often devastating economic reasons but because, being old, she "naturally" resists change (blame the victim). In fact, for an old woman, displacement means moving away from people for whom she has some continuous identity as a real person to a new neighborhood where she is seen simply as that nobody, "oldwoman." Perhaps I learned most about ageism when a woman in her sixties told me of her fear of leaving younger friends for too long a period. If they saw her frequently, they would continue to see her as herself. But she believed that if she were gone for awhile, and returned with more lifelines or other marks of aging, they might withdraw or treat her differently.

The women in Matthews' book express little direct anger. To ask why makes as much sense as asking why a battered wife stays with her husband. Dependency for survival on those whom you might alienate by your anger, absence of a support system, daily invalidation. And of course, "complaining" has conveniently been made part of the stigma of old age.[3]

A far more serious stigma, because more deeply buried —and not in Western culture alone—is the Evil Old Woman. Representing men's ancient and unconscious fear of women's power over death, the Evil Old Woman is the loathsome witch who cares only for herself and poisons and devours the young. Hence, the safest identity for an old woman is Grandmother, whose primary motive for living is to love and nourish the young. Grandmother is at best a third-hand identity, but it can serve to ward off active persecution.

And so we hear these women struggling to explain their oppression without betraying any hostility toward the young. "You know the younger people. They have their ways of doing." Or "I don't feel at home with younger people. They're nice and I love them and I love to watch them enjoy themselves, but I don't mix with them." The old woman who was called "ugly, ugly, ugly" adds, "I have to laugh about it now."

Matthews wrote her book to raise the consciousness of other sociologists and "professionals" as well as of lay people. It is to her credit that she is aware of how sociological methodologies intensify Otherness. I believe that these women would have revealed even more in response to questioning that was less "unbiased," more spontaneous and searching. And her book could have done more to point up the daily heroism that I see in the lives of old women, the depth of survival knowledge, and often a special inventiveness and creativity. But it is a tribute to Matthews that the quoted words of the women, in the context in which she places them, reverberate for us in new ways and stir questions that extend beyond her analysis.

By her limited choice of subject, Matthews excludes the special dimensions that aging and ageism have had for lesbians, or for women from Black, Jewish, Hispanic, North American Indian, or Asian American cultures. More serious is the fact that she does not acknowledge these limitations or speculate on how they may affect her findings. For example, I suspect that repression of anger may be more deeply ingrained in these heterosexual, white, presumably non-Jewish women who have spent their lives without words for oppression and who are currently unseen by the "women's" movement. The virtually unexplored territory of the triple impact of ageism, sexism, and racism on old women remains untouched in this book. As do different traditions and cultural attitudes towards age.

Across cultural lines, however, the heterosexual family and its extensions have almost always constituted the social world of old women. (In fact, until recently in the United States, women worn out with childbirth were often dead before the last child left home.) Most of Matthews' interviewees can depend on some moral support and services from daughters and daughters-in-law. A more vital family support system—including "fictive kin"[4]—seems to remain for minority women especially in relatively stable neighborhoods.

But the male-defined model of family, with its deep ambivalences and narrowly defined roles, is not a very adequate response to ageism and can, in fact, perpetuate it. (Even if all of the younger people on the block call you "grandma," you are still cast in a role with special expectations.) Indeed, given choices, even the choice of isolation, old women —including women from cultures where the bonds of blood are highly valued as a survival strategy—choose not to live with family. In Kramer and Masur's interviews,[5] women spoke with approval of the Jewish traditional wisdom that "if you live with children, you bring sin on them because you give them a chance to fight with their parents." In a rare article on old Black women, Jacqueline Johnson Jackson found that her interviewees preferred "intimacy at a distance" with their children and grandchildren.[6] Although the women in Matthews' book live alone, the need in an ageist society to rely on children for acceptance or essential services (present or projected) results in a profoundly unbalanced power relationship, in which the old woman must often bend to her children's definition of herself or comply with their wishes against her own best judgment. For the lesbian of any culture, relying on family to affirm her identity is even more problematic. Age cannot continue to be seen as a disease that only family, or even pseudo-family, can tolerate.

Matthews also fails to stress sufficiently the physical menace in the daily life of old women, the ever-present threat of assault. To be increasingly viewed with contempt by men proves no safeguard against rape. To be less physically strong and agile—or even to be perceived as such—makes us ready targets for male violence. Several old women I know express their increasing awareness of how power is acted out on the sidewalk. Who moves over for whom? A woman in Matthews' book describes being threatened by children with a stick. Another woman comments:

> You know about young people, but I don't pay any attention to them. Go over here to K-Mart and they take up the whole sidewalk. And the way they look at you, they wouldn't get off that sidewalk. You have to go around them...I don't like to go over there on Saturday or even late Friday afternoon because school's out.

Matthews refers to such encounters as "potentially demeaning situations." But in fact they are demeaning situations that are potentially violent. To mail your social security check to the bank, as old people are urged to do, may protect the check. It does not protect you when you want to walk out to visit a friend. All women are under a curfew; for the women in this book, and for the old women I know, the curfew begins much earlier and ends much later. Male violence, which so powerfully controls young, physically strong women's lives, is an even more powerful social control of old women.

To begin to understand ageism is to recognize that it is a point of convergence for many other repressive forces. The violence of men against women and against weaker, less powerful men. The lifelong economic and social status of women. Capitalism's definition of productivity and who can engage in it, and its indifference to those it forces to be "unproductive." Contempt for the physically challenged. Enforced and institutionalized heterosexuality and the family, which confine women to male-defined roles and economic dependencies. And inevitably racism—41% of Black women aged 65 or over lived in poverty in 1977, while 8% of white men in this age group were poor.

As we examine ageism, however, we must also recognize that it is a powerful force in itself, one deeply rooted in Western man's unconscious fears. Ageism reflects his sense of alienation from nature and her processes—especially childbirth and death, his association of these natural proc esses with woman, and his need to control both them and her.

Matthews' book is not tuned to such resonances, is more concerned with breaking down the stereotypes. She sees these stereotypes as existing only at this moment in history—accidental fallout from the Social Security legislation (enacted to deal with a shrinking job market) and Medicare (enacted by liberals who hoped it would be a first step towards National Health Insurance). These acts, she claims, equated "over 65" with "too old to work," physically and mentally sick, and useless. People over 65 were then no longer seen as "normal" people and became outcasts from the rest of society. Certainly in other countries and cultures where old women and men can continue active participation in their society, age has been less isolating and demeaning. But my reading does not support the idea that ageism is an overnight invention or one peculiar to the United States.

As the numbers of old people—especially old women —rapidly mulitply, we see a return to "family values" (meaning the free services of middle-aged daughters and daughters-in-law and the old woman's loss of autonomy) as the solution to the "problem of aging." We also see the beginnings of the large-scale exploitation of age for commercial and professional gain. That industry is not springing up to serve the interests of women.[7] And just as male obstetricians took control of childbirth, and male doctors and funeral directors took control of dying and death (also once women's province), male professionals and manufacturers are eager to control our relationship to aging.

It's time to refuse to let men define either the social world of old women or our life process. We need to build a vision of our own—one that goes beyond either commercial exploitation or the patchwork "solutions" of family. We need to reclaim the value and meaning of our entire lifespans up to and including death. But first we must examine the ageism in ourselves. Sarah Matthews' book is a good starting place.

–1982

Notes

[1]Two short stories, Alice Walker's "Everyday Use" (*In Love and Trouble*, Harcourt Brace Jovanovich, 1973) and Jan Clausen's "Yellow Jackets" (*Mother, Sister, Daughter, Lover*, Crossing Press, 1980) provide unusually perceptive commentary on the fetishizing of the old woman—the younger woman's tendency to romanticize the old woman's past while remaining uninterested in her current reality.

[2]In fact, there are few books at all that focus seriously on aging. One notable exception, which deals with both men and women, is Barbara Myerhoff's *Number Our Days* (Simon and Schuster, 1978), an invaluable resource on both aging and Jewish life.

[3]"They weren't cranky old people at all. They didn't even complain when my son's rock band practiced in the garage," said a neighbor to a reporter, describing a 68-year-old woman and her 79-year-old brother who had been shot in their beds. (*Boston Globe*, July, 31, 1982).

[4]Harriette Pipes McAdoo uses this term in discussing the networks in the Black community which interpret "family" far more flexibly. (*The Black Woman*, ed. La Frances Rodgers-Rose, Sage, 1980). North American Indian culture also widely expands the idea of family. See Beverly Hungry Wolf's *The Ways of My Grandmothers* (Morrow Quill, 1980).

[5]*Jewish Grandmothers*, Beacon, 1976.

[6]"The Plight of Older Black Women in the United States," *The Black Scholar* 7, 1976.

[7]In "Exploitation by Compassion" (*Broomstick*, Sept.-Oct. 1982, reprinted from *Equal Times*, 1980), Barbara Macdonald traces how society is geared up to increase the exploitation of the middle-aged woman's unpaid labor in the home and the young woman's poorly paid labor in institutions to "care for" the old woman—to the benefit of none of these women and for the profit of men.

An Open Letter to the Women's Movement

Barbara

I wrote this letter in response to a questionnaire sent to me by a university women's center that was developing a service for lesbians over 65. When I first held the questionnaire in my hand, I saw that its 165 questions were already defining me as an unknown curiosity. It had been five years since I wrote "Do You Remember Me?" and it seemed that nothing had changed. I decided to make my response an open letter because of the ageism that continued to remain, undealt with, in the entire women's community.

I have received your questionnaire for lesbians over 65 with the description of your proposed service, and I am pleased that your university is committed to dealing with ageism in the lesbian community. What follows, then, is not so much a criticism of your individual effort, but of the larger women's community: our years of neglect of the older woman, and our unwillingness to recognize and work on our own ageism with the same vigor that we have worked to eradicate sexism and racism. Any organization with the courage to make a start must inherit the problems resulting from this neglect—neglect by the women's movement and by the lesbian community. The problems cited here are ours, not yours.

Your service promises to bring older lesbians out of "their often self-imposed isolation so that their needs can be met, their problems solved, and their accomplishments recognized by an appropriate service organization." To fulfil this purpose, you foresee providing services such as "sympathetic visiting," "protective escorts," "bereavement support" and a "congenial meeting site for those lonely and depressed, where they can make new social contacts."

My first gut response is to say that as an old lesbian, I do not want to be addressed as "them." I don't want my problems solved for me, I don't want sympathy, and I don't want my accomplishments recognized by an appropriate service organization.

As a social worker who has worked many years in social agencies, I am dismayed that, in 1982, women can envision a program for old lesbians so much in the spirit of traditional social services—which have always separated women into the able and the needy. Surely we know that these services are set up to cover over, not change, the failures of the system; that they hire women not to empower their sisters, but rather to keep them forever at the other end of the "helping" service. Surely we know, in 1982, how the welfare mother is trapped, devalued, and exploited by the agencies that claim to be "helping" her with "her" problems. But apparently we are still so unaware of our ageism that we slip easily into the role of the able, helpful one and define the old woman as unable and needing help with "her" problems.

Your enclosure clearly implies that most lesbians over 65 are "incapacitated" (a word that insults the physically challenged woman of any age) and that the rest of us are lonely, depressed, bereaved, and probably need advice about our wills. Such stereotyping is offensive and segregating. SAGE (Senior Action in a Gay Environment) in New York City, the model for your proposed organization, estimates an active membership of approximately 250 gay men and women who go through their center in a month. Of those receiving services because they are homebound, they estimate fewer than 25 women. Many lesbians 20, 30, and 40 years old are physically challenged or lonely or depressed or bereaved or dying of cancer and need advice about their wills. Thus it seems misleading to segregate lesbians over 65 and address "them" from the point of view of "their" neediness. Why just us? Why not set up a service for all lesbians, and if those of us over 65 need the services provided for all, we will use them. If you think that lesbians over 65 won't come because we are suffering from self-imposed isolation, just put a few old lesbians in leadership roles, along with lesbians of all ages, and see what happens.

It is not my intent to single out for blame either your agency or SAGE. The description, the language used, is all too familiar, and could be used to describe most of the traditional, patch-up services found in the larger community. Publishing such descriptions of the oppressed group as unable to meet their own needs maintains the hierarchy of the service organization who serves them, whether they do so for salaries, grants, recognition, or out of a gratifying spirit of altruism—and it gives the service organization no incentive to eliminate the sources of the oppression.

Is that the best that the lesbian community can offer? We are a small community, less rigid, our institutions newer, more flexible, our prejudices (we can hope) less entrenched. We have both the vision and the will to eradicate prejudice at the source, not cover it up or patch it up. Consciousness raising, our method of getting at the source of prejudice, has been successful in making inroads into our sexism and our racism. We may not yet have been able to effect the changes we would like to see in the larger community, but we have begun to take care of the first piece of business—the sexism and racism in ourselves. Through consciousness raising, we have been encouraged to feel our anger, and this has empowered us to take charge of our own lives and to enter into leadership within our own organizations.

White women were slow to recognize our own racism in the women's movement (and in the lesbian movement), and we made a lot of mistakes. We sat in workshops and large conferences and described ourselves as *the* women's movement. We talked of doing something about racism. We went so far as to invite a few militant Black women to policy-making meetings as speakers to explain our own racism to us. And when these few women refused to be tokens, we said that we didn't know any other women of color and we couldn't find any.

But there were a lot of mistakes we didn't make in dealing with our sexism and our racism. Even though we recognized that most of us were poor and deprived of opportunity, we didn't follow the methods of the larger community by gathering old clothes. We didn't set up groups to deliver turkeys at Christmas. White women didn't approach the problem of our racism by setting up consciousness raising groups for Black women. White women didn't set up women's centers for women of color that were separate but equal. We didn't tell them that their oppression was self-imposed or organize bountiful ladies to solve their problems for them.

So why do we now go back to such obsolete methods for solving our own ageism? Those methods breed the same evils they always did—they stereotype, segregate, patronize, and stigmatize. They blame the victim, then having blamed her, they set up services to change her, solve her problems and meet her needs, then they pity her, and finally—I must point out—they exploit her.

Even with the best of intentions, traditional services get caught up in blaming the victim because the success or failure of the service depends upon producing change. The oppressor is very resistant to change and often unaware of being the source of the oppression. But the oppressed are much more vulnerable to intervention, and this soon gets equated with the need for the oppressed to change. Which is soon equated with somehow not doing it right—like "their self-imposed isolation."

I don't believe the oppression of Jews or people of color is self-imposed. And I don't think my oppression as an old lesbian is self-imposed. I have no difficulty in locating the sources of it—in the larger, patriarchal society, in the women's community, and in the lesbian community.

Briefly, let's examine the women's movement and ask ourselves some questions. How many women over 65 attend rallies, workshops, readings? How many over 60? Over 50? Where are we? Why don't we come? Before we start blaming the victim, maybe we ought first to ask, "What is really there for older women?"

Let's look at our publications. I subscribe to nine—three are lesbian, the others are radical feminist journals and newspapers. I know of only one that has pursued an outrageous, over-65 woman to join their editorial staff to raise consciousness about ageism or to edit out some of their published ageist material.

Your enclosure with the questionnaire speaks of first having to locate and get data on lesbians over 65. That reminds me of the reasons the all-white women's movement used to give for not including Black women in our planning and leadership—we couldn't find any, we didn't know any. Only now as we begin to see able, verbal, creative women of color throughout the lesbian and women's community, are white women forced to recognize that they were always there but we had made them invisible.

The Second Wave, a feminist magazine, recently ran an ad saying that they wished to add women of color to their collective, which they described as "diverse in our class backgrounds and ages." So I called in order to find out about the older women in their collective and learned that they had one woman who is 31 and that they had once had a woman who was 40. That's invisibility.

Nor did the women of *The Second Wave* come by this curious notion of age on their own. Probably one of their earliest impressions of what the women's movement is all about would have come from *Sisterhood is Powerful*, edited by Robin Morgan in 1970, which included 44 articles and 14 poems on all aspects of women's oppression. This very excellent anthology has one article on ageism, "It Hurts To Be Alive and Obsolete: The Aging Woman," by Zoe Moss. Moss, 43, writes: "I am bitter and frustrated and wasted, but don't you pretend for a minute as you look at me, forty-three, fat, and looking exactly my age, that I am not as alive as you are and that I do not suffer from the category into which you are forcing me." Should we be surprised that *The Second Wave* felt they had an old woman in their collective?

To read our publications through the eyes of an old woman, is to see the need for the active participation of women over 65 on their editorial staffs. By far the most glaring offense of almost all of them is the omission of any articles that address old women. The way in which this omission contributes to the invisibility of old women is beyond measure. But the editors also need to become more aware of the unconscious ageism in the material they publish.

A few examples from the most recent issues of our publications. In a dialogue on sexuality in one quarterly, not only is the sexuality of older women never addressed, but one of the speakers explains: "I went to live with my seventy-year-old grandmother. She was not the sweet-little-old lady type." Such stereotyping is offensive to me; perhaps the offensiveness will become more evident if you substitute Jew or Black—"the aggressive, rich Jew type" or "the happy-go-lucky Black type"—stereotypes this journal would never be guilty of.

In another quarterly, I find a story in which, not only the fictional narrator, but the story itself, assumes that the narrator's mother exists solely to serve as witness to her daughter's bravery and heroism. Such assumptions perpetuate attitudes that are destructive to older women.

In yet another journal, a letter is published as a model for other women to use. The attitude of the 40-year-old writer of this letter toward her 80-year-old aunt, who she hopes will send her money, is exploitative and insulting and renders the older woman invisible. I find it incomprehensible that the editors were so insensitive as to publish it.

This "model" letter suggests that younger women write old women relatives for money and that old women relatives include them in their wills. But the writer is not alone in this. Your own proposed organization offers to help old lesbians with their wills, and your questionnaire asks the old lesbian to list the amount of her income and the sources. I make no accusation. But when I then find that SAGE sends out flyers to their membership saying, "You can also support SAGE, Inc., by including us in your will," along with the suggested wording for such a bequest—it is time for our entire community to take a good look at what we are doing.

Stereotyping and segregation do not just end with innocent, unconscious prejudice. We segregated Black people and exploited their labor. We segregated Japanese Americans during World War II, and then took their businesses, their lands, and their other property. Stereotyping and segregation eventually lead to exploitation.

It is not any of the particulars of your proposed service that I object to. Women of all ages are homebound, sick, dying, and certainly that is also true of lesbians over 65. Women of any age can be killed in an automobile accident tomorrow, and there is nothing wrong with providing legal services to advise all women about their wills and to remind all women of the needs of the women's or lesbian community in making out their wills. My objection to your service is only in the segregated way you are beginning, and the implications about lesbians over 65 that can be drawn from such a beginning.

I can support a strong organization, coordinated out of your university, committed to stamping out ageism in the feminist and lesbian community—a community that is contributing to the "loneliness and depression" of the old lesbians that you speak of. If your organization is committed to empowering old lesbians, working actively to make us visible in positions of leadership, you won't need to "locate *them*" and "gather descriptive data about *them*." You will know us.

As a beginning, I would suggest that your university women's center:

1. Organize consciousness raising groups, a process in which old lesbians should be visible.

The women's movement has given lip service to opposing ageism, but no real work has ever been done to raise the consciousness of women about ageism enough for us to even recognize it.

2. Take leadership in insisting that the National Women's Studies Association devote an annual meeting to the issue and commit themselves to long-range plans for combatting ageism in every field study.

3. Set up an ongoing group assigned to monitor feminist and lesbian publications and to address the editors, requesting retractions of published ageist material. Not only would editing staffs become more aware, but the publishing of such letters would increase the awareness of a much larger population—their readers.

The following are a few suggestions to all of us for working on our ageism:

1. Don't expect that older women are there to serve you because you are younger—and *don't think the only alternative is for you to serve us.*

2. Don't continue to say "the women's movement," as I have in this letter, until all the invisible women are present—all races and cultures, and *all ages* of all races and cultures.

3. Don't believe you are complimenting an old woman by letting her know that you think she is "different from" (more fun, more gutsy, more interesting than) other older women. To accept the compliment, she has to join in your rejection of old women.

4. Don't point out to an old woman how strong she is, how she is more capable in certain situa-

tions than you are. Not only is this patronizing, but the implication is that you admire the way she does not show her age, and it follows that you do not admire the ways in which she does, or soon will, show her age.

5. If an old woman talks about arthritis or cataracts, don't think old women are constantly complaining. We are just trying to get a word in edgewise while you talk and write about abortions, contraception, pre-menstrual syndromes, toxic shock, or turkey basters.

6. Don't feel guilty. You will then avoid us because you are afraid we might become dependent and you know you can't meet our needs. Don't burden us with *your* idea of dependency and *your* idea of obligation.

7. By the year 2000, approximately one out of every four adults will be over 50. The marketplace is ready now to present a new public image of the aging American, just at it developed an image of American youth and the "youth movement" at a time when a larger section of the population was young. Don't trust the glossy images that are about to bombard you in the media. In order to sell products to a burgeoning population of older women, they will tell you that we are all white, comfortably middle class, and able to "pass" if we just use enough creams and hair dyes. Old women are the single poorest minority group in this country. Only ageism makes us feel a need to pass.

8. Don't think that an old woman has always been old. She is in the process of discovering what 70, 80, and 90 mean. As more and more old

women talk and write about the reality of this process, in a world that negates us, we will all discover how revolutionary that is.

9. Don't assume that every old woman is not ageist. Don't assume that I'm not.

10. If you have insights you can bring to bear from your racial background or ethnic culture—bring them. We need to pool all of our resources to deal with this issue. But don't talk about your grandmother as the bearer of your culture—don't objectify her. Don't make her a museum piece or a woman whose value is that she has sacrificed and continues to sacrifice on your behalf. Tell us who she is now, a woman in process. Better yet, encourage *her* to tell us.

I wish you luck in your beginning. We are all beginning.

–1982

Note

Zoe Moss' essay "It Hurts to be Alive and Obsolete: The Aging Woman," appears on p. 170 of *Sisterhood is Powerful* (New York: Vintage, 1970), ed. Robin Morgan.

The Women in the Tower

Cynthia

In April, 1982 a group of Black women demand a meeting with the Boston Housing Authority. They are women between the ages of sixty-six and eighty-one. Their lives, in the "housing tower for the elderly" where they live, are in continual danger. "You're afraid to get on the elevator and you're afraid to get off," says Mamie Buggs, sixty-six. Odella Keenan, sixty-nine, is wakened in the nights by men pounding on her apartment door. Katherine Jefferson, eighty-one, put three locks on her door, but "I've come back to my apartment and found a group of men there eating my food."

The menace, the violence, is nothing new, they say. They have reported it before, but lately it has become intolerable. There are pictures in the *Boston Globe* of three of the women, and their eyes flash with anger. "We pay our rent, and we're entitled to some security," says Mamie Buggs. Two weeks ago, a man attacked and beat up Ida Burres, seventy-five, in the recreation room. Her head wound required forty stitches.

"I understand your desire for permanent security," says Lewis Spence, the BHA representative. "But I can't figure out any way that the BHA is going to be offering 24-hour security in an elderly development." He is a white man, probably in his thirties. His picture is much larger than the pictures of the women.

The headline in the *Boston Globe* reads, "Elderly in Roxbury building plead with BHA for 24-hour security." Ida Burres is described in the story as "a feisty, sparrow-like woman with well-cared for gray hair, cafe au lait skin and a lilting voice." The byline reads "Viola Osgood." The story appears on page 19.

I feel that in my lifetime I will not get to the bottom of this story, of these pictures, of these words.

Feisty, sparrow-like, well-cared for gray hair, cafe au lait skin, lilting voice.

Feisty. Touchy, excitable, quarrelsome, like a mongrel dog.[1] "Feisty" is the standard word in newspaperspeak for an old person who says what she thinks. As you grow older, the younger person sees your strongly felt convictions or your protest against an intolerable life situation as an amusing over-reaction, a defect of personality common to mongrels and old people. To insist that you are a person deepens the stigma of your Otherness. Your protest is not a specific, legitimate response to an outside threat. It is a generic and arbitrary quirkiness, coming from the queer stuff within yourself—sometimes annoying, sometimes quaint or even endearing, never, never to be responded to seriously.

Sparrow-like. Imagine for a moment that you have confronted those who have power over you, demanding that they do something to end the terror of your days and nights. You and other women have organized a meeting of protest. You have called the press. Imagine then opening the newspaper and seeing yourself described as "sparrow-like." That is no simple indignity, no mere humiliation. The fact that you can be described as "sparrow-like" is in part why you live in the tower, why nobody attends. Because you do not look like a natural person—that is, a young or middle-aged person—you look like a sparrow. The real sparrow is, after all, a sparrow and is seen merely as homely, but a woman who is sparrow-like is unnatural and ugly.

A white widow tells of smiling at a group of small children on the street and one of them saying, "You're ugly, ugly, ugly." It is what society has imprinted on that child's mind: to be old, and to look old, is to be ugly, so ugly that you do not deserve to live. Crow's feet. Liver spots. The media: "I'm going to wash that gray right out of my hair and wash in my 'natural' color." "Get rid of those unsightly spots." And if you were raised to believe that old is ugly, you play strange tricks in your own head. An upper middle class white woman, a woman with courage and zest for life, writes in 1982: "When we love we do not see our mates as the young view us—wrinkled, misshapen, unattractive." But then she continues: "We still retain, somewhere, the *memory* of one another as beautiful and lustful, and we see each other at our *once-best.*"[2]

Old is ugly and unnatural in a society where power is male-defined, powerlessness disgraceful. A society where natural death is dreaded and concealed, while unnatural death is courted and glorified. But old is ugliest for women. A white woman newscaster in her forties remarks to a sportscaster who is celebrating his sixtieth birthday: "What women really resent about men is that *you* get more attractive as you get older." A man is as old as he feels, a woman as old as she looks. You're ugly, ugly, ugly.

Aging has a special stigma for women. When our wombs are no longer ready for procreation, when our vaginas are no longer tight, when we no longer serve men, we are unnatural and ugly. In medical school terminology, we are a "crock"; in the language of the street, we are an "old bag." The Sanskrit word for widow is "empty." But there is more than that.

Sparrow-like. The association of the old woman with a bird runs deep in the male unconscious. Apparently, it flows back to a time when men acknowledged their awe of what they were outsiders to—the interconnected, inseparable mysteries of life and death, self and other, darkness and light. Life begins in genital darkness, comes into light, and returns to darkness as death. The child in the woman's body is both self and other. The power to offer the breast is the power to withhold it. The Yes and the No are inextricable. In the beginning was the Great Mother, mysteriously, powerfully connected to the wholeness of Nature and her indivisible Yeses and Nos. But for those outside the process, the oneness was baffling and intolerable, and the Great Mother was split. Men attempted to divide what they could not control—nature and women's relationship to it. The Great Mother was polarized into separate goddesses or into diametrically opposed aspects of a single goddess. The Good Mother and the Terrible Mother. The Good Mother created life, spread her bounty outward, fertilized the crops, nourished and protected, created healing potions. The Terrible Mother, the original old Witch, dealt in danger and destruction, devoured children as food for herself, concocted poisons. Womb ≠ tomb, light ≠ darkness, other ≠ self. A world of connectedness was split down the middle.

The Terrible Mother was identified with the winged creatures that feed on mammals: vultures, ravens, owls, crows, bats. Her images in the earliest known culture of India show her as old, birdlike, hideous: "Hooded with a coif or shawl, they have high, smooth foreheads above their staring circular eye holes, their owl-beak nose and grim slit mouth. The result is terrifying...the face is a grinning skull."[3]

Unable to partake of the mystery of wholeness represented by the Great Mother, men first divided her, then wrested more and more control of her divided powers. The powerful Good Mother—bounteous life-giver, creator and nurturer of others—became the custodian of children who "belong" to the man or the male state. She can no longer even bear "his" child without the guiding forceps or scalpel of a man. She is the quotidian cook (men are the great chefs) who eats only after she has served others. She is the passive dispenser—as nurse, mother, wife—of the "miracles" of modern medicine created by the brilliance of man.

The Terrible Mother—the "old Woman of the West," guardian of the dead—represented men's fear of the powerful aspect of woman as intimate not only with the mysteries of birth but also of death. Today men are the specialists of death—despite a recent study that suggests that men face natural death with much more anxiety than women do.[4] Today male doctors oversee dying, male priests and rabbis perform the rituals of death, and even the active role of laying out the dead no longer belongs to woman (now the work of male undertakers). Woman is only the passive mourner, the helpless griever. And it is men who vie with each other to invent technologies that can bring about total death and destruction.

The Terrible Mother—the vulture or owl feeding on others— represented the fear of death, but also the fear of woman as existing not only to create and nurture others but to create and nurture her Self. Indeed, the aging woman's body is a clear reminder that women have a self that exists not only for others; it descends into her pelvis as if to claim the womb-space for its own. Woman's Self—her meeting of her own needs, seen by men as destructive and threatening—has been punished and repressed, branded "unnatural" and "unwomanly."

In this century, in rural China, they had a practice called "sunning the jinx." If a child died, or there was some similar misfortune, it was seen as the work of a jinx. The jinx was always an old, poor woman, and she was exposed to the searing heat of the summer sun until she confessed. Like the witches burned throughout Europe in the fifteenth to seventeenth centuries, she was tortured by doublethink. If she died without confessing, they had eliminated the jinx. If she confessed her evil powers, she was left in the sun for three more days to "cure her."[5] In Bali today, the Terrible Mother lingers on in magic plays, as Ranga, the witch who eats children, "a huge old woman with drooping breasts and a mat of white hair that comes down to her feet." It is a man who plays her part, and he must be old since only an old man can avoid the evil spirit of the Terrible Mother.[6]

In present-day white culture, men's fear of the Terrible Mother is managed by denial: by insisting on the powerlessness of the old woman, her harmless absurdity and irrelevance. The dread of her power lingers, reduced to farce—as in the Hansel and Gretel story of the old witch about to devour the children until the boy destroys her, or in the comic juxtaposition of Arsenic and Old Lace. The image of her winged power persists, totally trivialized, in the silly witch flying on her broomstick, and in "old bat," "old biddy," "old hen," "old crow," "crow's feet," "old harpy." Until, in April of 1982, an old woman's self-affirmation, her rage at her disempowerment, her determination to die naturally and not at the hands of men, can be diminished to feistiness, and she can be perceived as sparrow-like.

Sparrow-like. Writing for white men, did Viola Osgood unconsciously wish to say, "Ida Burres is not a selfish vulture—even though she is doing what old women are not meant to do, speak for their own interests (not their children's or grandchildren's but their own). She is an innocent sparrow, frail and helpless"? Or had she herself so incorporated that demeaning image—sparrow-like—that she saw Ida Burres through those eyes? Or both?

Well-cared for gray hair. Is that about race? About class? An attempt to dispel the notion that a poor Black woman is unkempt? Would Viola Osgood describe a Black welfare mother in terms of her "well-groomed afro"? Or does she mean to dispel the notion that this *old* woman is unkempt? Only the young can afford to be careless about their hair, their dress. The care that the old woman takes with her appearance is not merely to reduce the stigma of ugly; often it is her most essential tactic for survival: it signals to the person who sees her, I am old, but I am not senile. My hair is gray but it is well-cared for. Because to be old is to be guilty of craziness and incapacity unless proven otherwise.

Cafe au lait skin. Race? Class? Age? Not dark black like Katherine Jefferson, but blackness mitigated. White male reader, who has the power to save these women's lives, you can't dismiss her as Black, poor, old. She is almost all right, she is almost white. She is Black and old, but she has something in common with the young mulatto woman whose skin you have sometimes found exotic and sensual. And she is not the power of darkness that you fear in the Terrible Mother.

A lilting voice. I try to read these words in a lilting voice: "I almost got my eyes knocked out. A crazy guy just came in here and knocked me down and hit me in the face. We need security." These words do not lilt to me. A woman is making a demand, speaking truth to power, affirming her right to live—Black, Old, Poor, Woman. Is the "lilting" to say, "Although her words are strong, although she is bonding with other women, she is not tough and dykey"? Is the "lilting" to say, "Although she is sparrow-like, although she is gray-haired, something of the mannerisms you find pleasing in young women remain, so do not ignore her as you routinely do old women"?

I write this not knowing whether Viola Osgood is Black or white. I know that she is a woman. And I know that it matters whether she is Black or white, that this is not a case of one size fits all. But I know that Black or white, any woman who writes news articles for the *Globe,* or for any mainstream newspaper, is mandated to write to white men, in white men's language. That any messages to women, Black or white, which challenge white men's thinking can at best only be conveyed covertly, subversively. That any messages of appeal to those white men must be phrased in ways that do not seriously threaten their assumptions, and that such language itself perpetuates the power men have assumed for themselves. And I know that Black or white, ageism blows in the wind around us and certainly through the offices of the *Globe.* I write this guessing that Viola Osgood is Black, because she has known that the story is important, cared enough to make sure the photographer was there. I write this guessing that the story might never have found its way into the *Globe* unless through a Black reporter. Later, I find out that she is Black, thirty-five.

And I think that Viola Osgood has her own story to tell. I think that I, white Jewish woman of fifty, still sorting through to find the realities beneath the lies, denials and ignorance of my lifetime of segregations, cannot write this essay. I think that even when we try to cross the lines meant to separate us as women—old and young, Black and white, Jew and non-Jew—the seeds of division cling to our clothes. And I think this must be true of what I write now. But we cannot stop crossing, we cannot stop writing.

Elderly in Roxbury building plead with BHA for 24-hour security. Doubtless, Viola Osgood did not write the headline. Ten words and it contains two lies—lies that routinely obscure the struggles of old women. *Elderly.* This is not a story of elderly people, it is the story of old women, Black old women. Three-fifths of the "elderly" are women; almost all of the residents of this tower are women. An old woman has half the income of an old man. One out of three widows —women without the immediate presence of a man—lives below the official poverty line, and most women live one third of their lives as widows. In the United States, as throughout the world, old women are the poorest of the poor. Seven percent of old white men live in poverty, forty-seven percent of old Black women. "The Elderly," "Old People," "Senior Citizens," are inclusive words that blot out these differences. Old women are twice unseen—unseen because they are old, unseen because they are women. Black old women are thrice unseen. "Elderly" conveniently clouds the realities of power and economics. It clouds the convergence of racial hatred and fear, hatred and fear of the aged, hatred and fear of women. It also clouds the power of female bonding, of these women in the tower who are acting together as women for women.[7]

Plead. Nothing that these women say, nothing in their photographs, suggests pleading. These women are angry, and if one can demand where there is no leverage—and one can—they are demanding. They are demanding their lives, to which they know full well they have a right. Their anger is clear, direct, unwavering. "Pleading" erases the force of their confrontation. It allows us to continue to think of old women, if we think of them at all, as meek, cowed, to be pitied, occasionally as amusingly "feisty," but not as outraged, outrageous women. Old women's anger is denied, tamed, drugged, infantilized, trivialized. And yet anger in an old woman is a remarkable act of bravery, so dangerous is her world, and her status in that world so marginal, precarious. Her anger is an act of insubordination—the refusal to accept her subordinate status even when everyone, children, men, younger women, and often other older women, assumes it. "We pay our rent, and we're entitled to some security." When will a headline tell the truth: Old, Black, poor women confront the BHA demanding 24-hour security?

The housing tower for the elderly. A tall building filled with women, courageous women who bond together, but who with every year are less able to defend themselves against male attack. A tower of women under seige. A ghetto within a ghetto. The white male solution to the "problem of the elderly" is to isolate the Terrible Mother,

That tower, however, is not simply architectural. Nor is the male violence an "inner city problem." Ten days later, in nearby Stoughton, a man will have beaten to death an eighty-seven-year-old white woman, leaving her body with "multiple blunt injuries around her face, head, and shoulders."[8] This woman was not living in a housing tower for the elderly. She lived in the house where she was born. "She was very, very spry. She worked in her garden a lot and she drove her own car," reports a neighbor. She had the advantages of race, class, a small home of her own, a car of her own. Nor did she turn away from a world that rejects and demeans old women ("spry," like "feisty," is a segregating and demeaning word). At the time of her murder, she was involved in planning the anniversary celebration at her parish.

Yet she was dead for a week before anyone found her body. Why? The reporter finds it perfectly natural. "She outlived her contemporaries and her circle of immediate relatives." Of course. How natural. Unless we remember de Beauvoir: "One of the ruses of oppression is to camouflage itself behind a natural situation since, after all, one cannot revolt against nature."[9] How natural that young people, or even the middle aged, should have nothing in common with an old woman. Unthinkable that she should have formed friendships with anyone who was not in her or his seventies or eighties or nineties. It is natural that without family, who must tolerate the stigma, or other old people who share the stigma, she would have no close ties. And it is natural that no woman, old or young, anywhere in the world, should be safe from male violence.

But it is not natural. It is not natural, and it is dangerous, for younger women to be divided as by a taboo from old women—to live in our own shaky towers of youth. It is intended, but it is not natural that we be ashamed of, dissociated from, our future selves, sharing men's loathing for the women we are daily becoming. It is intended, but it is not natural that we be kept ignorant of our deep bonds with old women. And it is not natural that today, as we re-connect with each other, old women are still an absence for younger women.

As a child—a golden-haired Jew in the segregated South while the barbed wire was going up around the Warsaw ghetto—I was given fairy tales to read. Among them, the story of Rapunzel, the golden-haired young woman confined to a tower by an old witch until she was rescued by a young prince. My hair darkened and now it is light again with gray. I know that I have been made to live unnaturally in a tower for most of my fifty years. My knowledge of my history—as a woman, as a lesbian, as a light-skinned woman in a world of dark-skinned women, as the Other in a Jew-hating world—shut out. My knowledge of my future—as an old woman— shut out.

Today I reject those mythic opposites: young/old, light/darkness, life/death, other/self, Rapunzel/Witch, Good Mother/Terrible Mother. As I listen to the voices of the old women of Warren Tower, and of my aging self, I know that I have always been aging, always been dying. Those voices speak of wholeness: To nurture Self = to defy those who endanger that Self. To declare the I of my unique existence = to assert the We of my connections with other women. To accept the absolute rightness of my natural death = to defend the absolute value of my life. To affirm the mystery of my daily dying and the mystery of my daily living = to challenge men's violent cheapening of both.

But I cannot hear these voices clearly if I am still afraid of the old witch, the Terrible Mother in myself, or if I am estranged from the real old women of this world. For it is not the wicked witch who keeps Rapunzel in her tower. It is the prince and our divided selves.

Note: There was no follow-up article on the women of the tower, but Ida Burres, Mamie Buggs, Mary Gordon, Katherine Jefferson, Odella Keenan, and the other women of Warren Tower, did win what they consider to be adequate security—"of course, it is never all that you could wish," said Vallie Burton, President of the Warren Tower Association. They won because of their own bonding, their demands, and also, no doubt, because of Viola Osgood.

–1983

Notes

The article from the *Boston Globe* on which this essay is based appeared on April 16, 1980, p. 19.

[1]ed. William Morris, *American Heritage Dictionary* (Boston: Houghton Mifflin, 1975).

[2]Harriet Robey, *There's a Dance in the Old Dame Yet* (New York: Atlantic-Little Brown, 1982), p. 170. Italics mine.

[3]Eric Neumann, *The Great Mother* (New York: Bollingen, 1972), p. 150. Neumann has collected the most wide-ranging evidence of the Good and Terrible Mothers in cultures as distant from each other as Peru, Egypt, and India.

[4]See Carol M. Schulz, "Age, Sex and Death Anxiety in a Middle-Class American Community," in *Aging in Culture and Society*, ed. Christine L. Fry (New York: J.F. Bergin, 1980), p. 246. According to her findings, old women's attitudes toward dying become increasingly positive and accepting, while "males become emotionally more negative toward approaching death."

[5]Annie Dillard, "For the Love of China" (*Harvard Magazine*, July–August, 1983, p. 41). Dillard describes reading about this custom of "sunning the jinx" in Shen Conquen's *Recollections of West Hunan*, translated by Gladys Yeng. Note the brutal use of a source of light—as in the fires built to consume European witches—to destroy the dark powers of the Terrible Mother.

[6]Simone de Beauvoir, *The Coming of Age* (New York: Putnam, 1972), p. 78.

[7]Several studies of public housing projects for the elderly reveal creative, fluid networks of practical and emotional support among the women. The men, on the other hand, tend to "emphasize impersonal and businesslike, including monetary, aspects" in their occasional assistance as handymen or chauffeurs. (Karen Jones and Edward Wellin,

"Dependency and Reciprocity: Home Health Aid in an Elderly Population," in Fry, *op. cit.*, p. 32). Middy Thomas, of the Mayor's Commission on the Elderly in Boston said of Warren Tower, "It's the women who do everything."

[8]*Boston Globe,* April 26, 1982, p. 13.

[9]Simone de Beauvoir, *The Ethics of Ambiguity* (New Jersey: Citadel, 1948), p. 83.

The Power of the Old Woman

Barbara

Valerie Taylor's novel *Prism,*[1] is probably the first of many we will be reading that will reflect the practical realities facing lesbians as we grow older. It is not, of course, the first novel written by a lesbian about aging. *Sister Gin*[2] was published in 1975, *As We Are Now* in 1973.[3] There is much to be gained by examining all three of these novels as each is, in itself, a singular way of approaching the whole problem of aging in a society that denies aging, denies death. A society which, in anticipation of the year 2000 (when one out of every four persons will be over 50), is planning a whole new image of aging that will tell us we are as young as we feel and that how to feel young is to look young. A society which is developing endless products to keep us looking young. Which is to say that society isn't going to let us grow old naturally any more than they have ever let a lesbian, or any other woman for that matter, do what comes naturally. Nor do I think we can really escape having a heterosexual image of aging forced on us in the next ten or twenty years. But I do think we will face the experience with a clearer vision if we let ourselves feel and experience our own aging now, so that we know some of its realities from our gut before we are deluged with messages from the market place that tell us what to feel.

It is clear from our own sparse literature that we are already reacting to society's attitude toward aging—that is, that old is ugly, old is powerless, old is the end, and therefore that old is what no one could possibly want to be.

At 69, I take in these messages from the outside every day, and I have had to learn ways of reacting to all the negative messages around me in order to survive. Some of my reactions are at a great cost to me, and some have taken me deeply into myself to a rich resource I might never have known was there. But deep experiences are not the everyday ones for any of us. In a day of living as an old woman, I reach for all the ways possible on that particular day, in that given moment—so that I feel none of the ways of reacting to oppression are wrong (old women, like all women, are trying to make it from day to day), but some ways are more to be sought after and worked for than others.

Prism is about one of those ways we respond to aging. Anne is 65 when we meet her in her Chicago three-room apartment in the early evening. She has just come home from her retirement party. The apartment is empty except for the packing boxes. Tomorrow she will leave early and drive her VW to an apartment she has never seen in upstate New York where rent will be cheaper. The questions she asks herself are real questions: How will I live on social security? What kind of clothes will I wear for the rest of my life since I'm never going to dress for work again? What will I do for fun if sex is over? How will I live alone if I am never to have another lover?

Anne arrives and finds her little two-room apartment over a hardware store. She goes to the senior citizen's lunches; she gets a part-time job in a grocery store; she meets Eldora. So her questions are answered—Yes, she can live on social security. Yes, she will have some kind of job. Yes, her sex life will continue, and Yes, she will find a lover. When you have carried a negative popular image around in your head all your life, as most of us have, who can resist turning it around in a positive way to prove the answer is Yes not No? All of the answers Valerie Taylor has given us are true in a sense but, in another sense, her answers are not true. Yet she feels forced to give them.

Proving that I'm still strong, capable, sexual, is a response I give to a negative world a dozen times a day. (Maybe that's the reason I enjoyed the book so much.) Like Valerie Taylor I am forced to. I can at least avoid invisibility that way. But perhaps it's inevitable that when we react to a stereotype, that reaction ricochets and we end up smack in the middle of another. *Prism* is a story that says, "You really are as young as you think you are."

But there is another, much more costly, response to invisibility which is easy to fall into—living in an age-fearing society invites it. That is the denial that says, "I'm not old, I'm just eccentric!" This kind of response to aging is not surprising as it has always been a common response of oppressed people. It is a forced response. The midget, the court jester, the Black funny man, the fat lady, the tramp—with his clothes that don't fit, smoking the thrown-away cigar, telling us that poverty and powerlessness are funny—all are responding to the oppressor who says entertain me, amuse me, deny in front of me, what I am doing to you daily. One has the moral choice to play to an audience who prefers the lie in the laugh, or to confront the oppressor with the truth that dwarfism is not funny, Black is not funny, fat is not funny, poverty and powerlessness are not funny, and old is not funny.

June Arnold's *Sister Gin* is in many ways a rich and delightful and daring novel. But in *Sister Gin* we are told that age is funny. Middle age (as we see it in Sue and Bettina, two lesbian lovers) is made up of hot flashes which can only be remedied by great quantities of cold gin, alternated with sexual desire which can only be satisfied in the arms of an old woman.

The denial of aging in *Sister Gin* can best be understood if we look at the ways in which women who have never had their consciousness raised deny their own oppression as women. In their need to deny, not only will they say that they have never experienced oppression and are not oppressed, but they may go all the way with their denial by turning it around and by saying that actually they are privileged and it is really men who suffer. We have a similar kind of turn-around in *Sister Gin,* in which the women in mid-life are depicted as crazy, funny, disorganized, unable to get along with each other, unable to get their act together, always complaining about their physical ailments, and the old women are also funny and crazy but nevertheless organized, united, more willing to take risks, and physically so strong that they can get together in the middle of the night, grab a rapist, tie him to a board and leave him nude for the townspeople to view in the morning. (Frankly, it is such a good story that I smile with remembered pleasure as I write this and nearly forget how ageist it is. But ageist it is.) *Sister Gin* not only tells us, "You're as young as you think you are," but that you are really younger than the middle aged or even the very young. It is, as is *Prism,* a strong Yes to society's No and, like *Prism,* it is both true and untrue.

In order to see the underlying truth in *Sister Gin,* it is necessary to approach the whole subject from a much deeper level of consciousness, and May Sarton has done this in *As We Are Now.* Caro, 76, is a retired teacher who is placed by her brother in an old, run-down nursing home in the country, with four old men and one young man who is retarded and spastic and who is tied in a chair. Caro lives in a tiny room adjacent to the old men; through the thin walls, she can hear them laughing and sneering at the caretaker's breasts. Angry at having to care for the old in order to make a living, the caretakers express their anger by dominating the old people. Caro struggles to survive the shock of being deserted there by hanging on to the values she has had all her life—reading, writing, listening to music—all of which further angers the caretakers who see her as a snob and who are determined to make her submissive.

In this beautifully crafted story, told through the voice of Caro's copybook, Sarton is telling us about the process of aging. Sarton is not caught up in denying society's No's; rather she meets them head on. She seems to be saying: I don't care whether you think old women are strong or not, powerful or not, young as they think they are or not. In fact, I will give you all of society's No's as a premise to my story. Caro is too old to be physically strong and powerful; and I am not going to try to prove to you that old women can do what they choose in the world. I am putting Caro in a small world that will grow smaller every day and in which she will experience greater and greater restriction, because I believe that to be a given in the aging process and it is not to be denied. I am going to give Caro only three friends who care about her, because having fewer people in your life is one of the realities of growing old. And those three friends will not desert her and leave her to die alone; Caro herself will finally leave them behind in a very conscious way because she has a task and a goal of her own that must take priority. That task is that she must take charge of her life and her own dying.

Because something in Caro will not be dominated, the caretakers, in their determination to drive her into submission and senility, turn away visitors and intercept her mail. They refuse to let her know the month or day of the week. But Caro sits in her room and watches out her window for the changing colors of the seasons, and in order to be sure that she is not losing her memory, keeps a copybook and records her daily experiences. She begins:

> I am not mad, only old. I make this statement to give me courage. To give you an idea of what I mean by courage, suffice it to say that it has taken two weeks for me to obtain this notebook and pen.

A minister and his young daughter come into Caro's narrowing world and give her some hope. Seeing the dirt and the neglect of the patients, the minister alerts the Health inspectors, although this only results in the caretakers' increased suspicion of Caro, and their greater determination to turn away visitors. However, in a way very different from Anne in *Prism,* Caro finds a lover. Indeed, it is out of the very restrictions of her life that Caro discovers a love that is capable of cutting across society's taboos of class and sexuality.

A farm woman, Anna, comes to take the caretakers' place when they go on vacation. She comes with warmth and caring. She cleans up the dirt, puts a cloth on the tray, brings flowers, and talks with Caro. For Caro, she is a "miracle...I am stretched out on my bed like a swimmer who, near exhaustion, can lie on a beach and rest at last."

The reprieve is not for long; the caretakers return. But Caro writes in her copybook:

> So I am busy making up letters. That is something to hold onto. How very strange that at seventy-six in a relationship with an inarticulate person who cannot put any of it into words, I myself

> am on the brink of understanding things about love I have never understood before... Have I ever before really understood the power and the healing grace of sensitive hands like Anna's? Have I ever experienced loving as I do in one glance from her amazing clear eyes that take in at once what my needs are, whether it be food or a gentle caress, a pillowcase changed, a glass of warm milk?

When Caro's mail is read by the caretakers, they use it to destroy her in new ways. One of the caretakers berates her, "I didn't know you were a dirty old woman... At least the old men think about women. They are not filthy like you." For Caro, who is fearful of losing her mind, the accusations of the "sickness" of lesbianism and the "sickness" of age become one. Love loses its power and joy; she feels that even Anna must have ridiculed her. Desperate, she tries to escape, but the caretakers come after her. They threaten her with commitment to the State Hospital, and Caro wonders if even that might be better. It is then that she recognizes that death—how to die—must be faced head on.

> There is a point of no return, a point when the only question is whether to choose to starve to death or to use a more violent means.

This, for Caro, is the beginning of her freedom. By the time the minister's daughter manages to take her to the farm to visit Anna, Caro sees that Anna's love is still there but that she herself has changed. She has a task to do, and "whatever powers I have must be concentrated on doing it soon."

Caro makes her plan to take action and she plans it well. The old men and the retarded boy are as hopelessly locked into the indifference and degradation as she, numbly awaiting the release of death. She is the only one who can still act. She knows that the caretakers are putting tranquilizers in her coffee and that she must fight to keep alert. She saves her lighter fluid, and when the minister's daughter brings a holiday wreath, which the caretaker takes from her to put on the front door, everybody wonders what happened to the candles. She knows that she must wait to act until the roads are impassable with snow so the fire engines cannot get through. She must make sure the cat is out.

> It is strange that now I have made my decision I can prepare for death in a wholly new way... I have believed since I came here that I was here to prepare for death, but I did not yet know how to do it. At first I felt I must cling to myself, keep my mind alive somehow—that was... a losing battle, for the best I could hope for was to stand still in the same place...
>
> I see, now that death is not a vague prospect but something I hold in my hand, that the very opposite is required from what I thought at first.

Caro lives suspended, the scales balanced, the desire to keep living (with the knowledge that at best that is standing still) on the one side, and the desire to take action—which is to live fully in the now but which will end her life—on the other. But she holds to her purpose, even when the minister announces, "We have got to get you out of here." Caro's last act before setting fire to the "home" is to place all of her copybooks in the frigidaire, a "testament" to the politics of her dying.

I suggested earlier that I thought *Prism* might be the beginning of a new genre in lesbian fiction in the next ten years. Today I walk into New Words Bookstore in Cambridge and see the shelves filled and realize that, with a few exceptions, our lives are not recorded there, only half our lives are there—our childhoods, our youths, our forties. The last half of our lives is unknown. I anticipate great changes in our short stories and novels as many lesbians begin to leave the work force and become categorized as "old." We will be getting our first social security check, or worse, not getting it. We will be going to a movie for the first time without adult status because it costs five dollars to be an adult and only two-fifty to be a child or a senior citizen—and we will realize that we can't afford adulthood. We will be wanting to write about these experiences. (And I hope to God wanting to do something about them.) And with many voices we will be answering the same questions that Anne asks in *Prism*: How will I live, what will I wear, will I live alone, will I find a lover? All good questions and we will need to find answers as we go on living our lives.

But it is undeniably true that we are all slowly moving in the direction that Caro describes. Perhaps not in our seventies, perhaps not in our eighties, but the process irrevocable. We will all finally think Caro's thoughts as our world narrows and our choices become fewer, until we have just one choice really, one sense of possibility, and so what matters is doing it well. In Caro's words,

> I am knotted up to a single purpose now. What a relief! I am stripped down to nothing, needing no protection anymore. All needs have been fulfilled. Is this madness, God?
>
> I believe it is close to it. But perhaps at the farthest reach and in the presence of death there is no distinction to be made. Absolute nakedness may be madness. It doesn't matter. It is what is *required.*

The process of aging has been hidden from us all our lives. We are told that with the help of modern medicine and technology old age isn't really necessary. One can have an active life right up to the "end." You are as young as you think you are. There are hair dyes to make your hair look its "natural color," creams to remove the wrinkles and brown spots, and with all of these no woman should look as though she is "failing"—she should look "well-preserved." But we always suspect that any process so well hidden has some kind of power. And indeed it has.

What is the power of the old woman? Some would suggest that it is her knowledge because she has lived longer. At 69, I can tell you that I don't know all that much, and when I try to tap this source of power in other old women I find that they don't know that much either. In Trikkala, Greece, the women who work in the fields say that for lack of child care they must leave their children with the grandmothers, and that the grandmothers have old ideas and do not recognize that the women are in the midst of a revolution; it takes the mothers hours each night to undo the unliberated ideas that the grandmothers have instilled during the day. Though it is by no means necessarily so, years of experience can also be years of brainwashing.

In *As We Are Now,* Sarton defines the power for us. Caro claims her power when she sees that the challenge is not how to live—the challenge is how to die. That is her direction, her purpose, her necessity. Caro is not afraid to die, so in a way never possible before she is not afraid to live.

This is the source of the old woman's power. This is the truth in the comic denials and exaggerations of *Sister Gin* (indeed, Arnold refers to *As We Are Now* in her novel, without absorbing its implications)—that the old woman is approaching a place of greater freedom and daring than she has ever been allowed to know before. For the first time in her life an old woman can refuse society's meaningless busywork and self-betrayals and she can take charge of her own life. Such a woman won't do what she is told, she will only do what is important to her own life direction.

From the day the old woman was born, society has been afraid that she would someday take charge of her own life. To make sure she would not, society kept her living on the edge, living with the ultimate fear of not surviving. Actual death was hidden from her. Even when she went to funerals to view death it was only after powders, creams, and dyes had been put on to make death look like life. Scrambling from day to day, always concentrating on survival, she was never allowed a moment for contemplation about the ultimate goal. She was born into a world that told her that her life was not her own. Your life is not your own if you can't take it. In moments of anger she would say to her mother, "I didn't ask to be here." And the mother was silenced by society not to reply, "No, but you can choose every day whether or not you want to stay." So from the beginning of the old woman's life she lost the chance to feel herself choose life by, as Caro says, "hold(ing) death in (her) hand." To be denied that choice is to be denied a powerful affirmation. To be denied that choice is to live half a life, a lifetime with only one foot in the door. It is to believe your life isn't your own, but something thrust upon you. There is a lack of morality in such a life which invites you not to take responsibility for the fact that you really do make the choice to live, and for what the terms of that choice are.

Does the power of the old woman have to come so late in life, often in our late eighties? Or can we draw on that power much sooner? The time I spend proving I am as young as I think I am is lost time. As Caro says, "at best just standing still in one place." On my best days, I live deeply with the knowledge that my choices are narrowing but that all my life they were much more narrowed when I bought into society's denial of death. My wrinkled face now reminds me of what the terms were every day of my life and on my best days, I agree to that contract in a moral way.

–1983

Notes

[1]Valerie Taylor, *Prism* (Tallahassee: Naiad Press, 1981).

[2]June Arnold, *Sister Gin* (Houston: Daughters, Inc., 1975).

[3]May Sarton, *As We Are Now* (New York: W. W. Norton, 1973).

Cynthia's Afterword

You and I are talking over cups of coffee in a restaurant. Suppose that, from time to time as we talk, we are aware that we grew up in different generations or that we may be facing different life experiences because of our ages. We can still talk freely and honestly. Sometimes our differences will be important, sometimes not. We can share and learn from those differences.

But if I carry in my head the notion that you are "young enough to be my daughter," or you are thinking, "she is old enough to be my grandmother," the quality of our dialogue is instantly converted. Our roles are defined for us; the possibility for real exchange between us is radically diminished.

Ageism is not a recent form of oppression, an evil that sprang up with the American youth culture. It is as old as the history of the family. Unless we understand that history, how it has served men and divided women, we cannot begin to deal with our individual ageism or succeed as a collective movement in eradicating it.

Men used family as a way of controlling individual women, and thereby of colonizing women as a class. Family was the original master-servant model. The English word "family" derives from the Latin *familia,* meaning: *Servants of a household, household including not only the servants but also the head of the household and all persons related to him by blood or marriage.* In old English law, "familia" meant "the servants of one master."

Familia is as clearly a male institution for controlling others who are subservient to the master's goals and values as was the plantation system of master, mistress, overseer, house slave, field slave. It is as much an economic unit as the corporation with its president, administrative assistant, secretary. In any of these institutions, it is the master who sets up the class system and decides just how those he has power over are to serve him. He makes clear separations of titles and roles among the servants, not only for efficiency in meeting his goals, but because these roles create divisions and prohibit free communication. The roles promise him that there will be no uprising. To step out of role—whether as secretary, or house slave, or grandmother—is to step out of the system and to question the master's authority.

The power and promise of the present women's movement depend on our freedom to exist, however precariously, outside of the system of familia. Instead of exchanging small strategies for survival, we have been able to imagine a world free from domination and to demand a voice in creating that world.

Despite all of this, in the past five years of the women's movement, many of us have felt compelled to return to familia. In response to our oppression as Jewish women, or Black or Asian American or North American Indian women, we go back to family to defend our individual cultures, to find a sense of self, and with the hope there will be some comfort there and some clarity. Clarity is surely needed when our cultures have been despised and often almost annihilated by another hostile, dominant culture, or when our families have been used as targets for racism or Jew hating.

Many of us return to familia in part to free ourselves for awhile from an oppressive culture and the false roles it imposes on us and on our families. But as we open the doors of our family homes, we need to see that we still impose on ourselves and on other women—inside and outside of our families—the old restraints of the oppressive roles of a class system. We need to know that our ageism began in familia, that we carried it with us when we left familia, and that we bring it back with us when we return.

We left familia with the master's brands on our foreheads, and they are still there. Younger woman = daughter. Older woman = mother. Old woman = grandmother. We see the brands before we look in each other's eyes. The brands remind us that, inside or outside of familia, we are, first and foremost, the servants of the master. The brands say that we will continue to be good servants—to police ourselves and to police each other, as good servants always do. We will hold each other to our roles. We will deny each other the subversive power that lies in possibilities.

Ageism was branded onto the women's movement with the word "Sisterhood." When we accepted Sisterhood we accepted that class system, with all of the mistrust and division the master had instilled between younger and older women. We dismissed mothers and grandmothers as outsiders to the action. We excluded older women from a struggle for freedom just as we had excluded our mothers and grandmothers from our whispered rebellions as daughters in the master's house. Once we had accepted the brand of Sisterhood, we could not even see how we had dismissed and excluded older women.

Del Martin and Phyllis Lyon describe unlearning "husband-and-wife" as lesbian lovers—discovering that they could free themselves from those roles, learned in familia. If we all unlearn our lessons well enough, we will someday be shocked to remember that we once saw older women as our "mothers," and old women as our "grandmothers." Or that young women began a movement for the liberation of all women by calling one another "sisters."

Today, as so many young women move out into a larger world—freed from familia by access to birth control and abortion—they see, if they are looking, more and more old women. These women have also been freed—accidentally, as it were, since Social Security was enacted to keep old men off the labor market—to choose a life outside of familia. They are impoverished: eighty-five percent of all old women who are single or widowed live near or below the poverty line. But they know familia well; most have spent six or seven decades behind its doors. And however tiny their incomes, one fact is clear: they are determined not to go back.

Each time we see such a woman as "grandmother," we dismiss the courage of her independence; we invalidate her freedom. We tell her, in the face of her own choice, that her real place is in the home.

And what does it really mean to define an old woman by her class status in familia? At different times, in different places, the master has assigned her different roles. Sometimes as policewoman to his son's wife (hence the bitter mother-in-law jokes); sometimes as instructor, to teach his wife and daughters the skills they need to serve him better.

But today the role required of her in familia is "grandmother." It does not matter to the master how much she may have longed for the day when she would be freed from children's demands; freed to listen not to their voices, but to her own. If she is indifferent to her grandchildren or impatient with them—if she is convinced that her own last years are just as important as their early ones—then her uselessness to the master threatens her very survival. She can be called senile, and tamed with drugs. To see an old woman as "grandmother" is to join the master in defining her as a woman whose right to exist depends on her loving and serving us.

A woman who lives outside of the male institution of family is indeed dangerous to men. If younger women refuse to join men in relegating her to the role of "grandmother"; if we insist that her forced labor in the home cannot be the only solution to her poverty; if we join her in resisting her deportation—and our own—back into familia, we will see the danger that she represents to male domination. And we will begin to have a movement, not of "sisters," but of all women.

This book represents Barbara's and my determination to break down the roles that have oppressed us and, in doing so, to challenge the class system that produced them. Only as women of all ages free ourselves from the master's house, can we sit down over cups of coffee and talk to each other as free and equal women.

Notes

The definitions of Family and Familia appear in *Webster's Third New International Dictionary of the English Language* (Springfield: G&C Merriam, 1976), pp. 821 and 820, respectively.

Del Martin and Phyllis Lyon describe their unlearning of roles in *Lesbian/Woman* (San Francsico: Glide Publications, 1972).

Barbara's Afterwords

It is now July of 1983 as Cynthia and I complete this collection of essays and reviews on aging. We have come to the Anza-Borrego Desert in California to live for a year in a trailer in a community of about ten people. Only five have remained for these hot summer months; the others will return in September. All of the residents live in mobile homes or trailers; most are in their late sixties, live alone, and have chosen the isolation of the desert. Most are women.

Away from the streets of Cambridge and the sights and sounds of a youthful community, I would have expected to be less aware of my own aging, but instead I am acutely aware: more aware because I am five years older than when I wrote "Do You Remember Me?"; because the glare of the desert on my cataracts makes my vision less clear; because every task I start in making small repairs on the trailer, for example (something I have always done easily and gotten satisfaction from), ends now in frustration and fury because I can't see; because I am much more aware of joint pain now, and on some days avoid walking on the uneven terrain of the desert.

But none of these changes is really constant. Even when I am frustrated by the glare in trying to get a screwdriver into the head of a screw, I am well aware that if I wait until the sun goes down behind the mountain, I will see the screw head clearly. And it is only on some days that I avoid walking on the uneven terrain, and I am never sure on which days I may notice the sharp pain and on which days I may not.

But daily I am taking in a sense of change and of loss. I grieve for my lost vision. Surgery may mean I will see and may even be able to drive for a few more years—but some part of the body my mother gave me is gone forever. It will never come back.

The pain I feel when I jar myself in walking is, no doubt, the result of bone loss and although I do not feel the pain often, I have the knowledge that I will never run again. I grieve with this new knowledge and realize that I cannot remember when I last ran. What I am always aware of, somewhere in the back of my mind but not taken out and examined as I do now on this page, is that I am in the process of dying and that all of this is a part of the life experience. One doesn't just die all of a sudden. It is a process and one we may be conscious of for the last ten or twenty years of our life, which if you think about it, may be a quarter or more of your lifetime. I find myself wondering why this is not more talked about and why it has not become the common knowledge of our lives.

I am self-conscious in writing this. For after all, no one speaks of dying until they have only a few months or weeks or hours to live. This is society's definition of dying. It asks that I deceive myself and others about my daily awareness that my body is using itself up; it prevents me from calling this process by name for myself and others.

Not only am I self-conscious, I also feel shame in talking about my bodily discomfort, aware of the stigma of "old people are always complaining." But the fact is we spend our lives conveying to others how we feel in our bodies. We all have a real need to communicate our body experience. It is the language of lovers. Babies and small children are either crying because something hurts or gurgling or giggling because something feels good. Adolescents and young adults are preoccupied with their bodies: "Am I going to be tall or am I going to be short? Am I too fat? Am I too thin? Are my breasts going to be too small or are my breasts going to be too big? I have had my period, or I have not had my period yet." Women discuss their bodies endlessly: "I am pregnant. I am not pregnant. I was in labor for days. I was only in labor for a few hours." And a few years later they are saying, "I am going through the change. I have not gone through the change yet. I am flashing. I am not flashing." Suddenly in my sixties, when my body is doing all kinds of things, sending me all kinds of messages, I am not supposed to talk about it.

The fact that I am not supposed to talk about the gradual process of dying, the fact that you who are younger have been taught to hear my bodily experience as complaining, the fact that I feel embarrassed to talk about my dying because it isn't in a year or a month or an hour—I can't dismiss all this as though it were just more evidence of ageism in our society. These distortions of our life experience are learned, they run deep and they are political.

I have to ask myself, "Why am I being silenced? What is the message that I have to tell you that you are forbidden to hear?"

I mention in "The Power of the Old Woman" how death was hidden from the old woman all her life, but as I write this afterword, I see that only some deaths were hidden from her: the deaths of other old women, the unseen deaths of the poor, the unspeakable deaths of Black women and Black men, the deaths of generations of women who died in childbirth. I see now that all my life, as in yours, one death was always visible in film, in art, and in literature—the agonizing death of the hero who dies gloriously in mortal combat, usually on the battlefield. We see him always in that single moment of dying.

He was recruited to battle out of his fear of death and his love of glory. "If we don't kill them, they will kill us" makes possible the escalation of armaments, territorial conquests, and eventually puts the power in the hands of a few. For this to succeed, death must be defined as a single event, not as a life process. It is that single event that war is supposed to save us from. Men in battle are portrayed as brave and fearless, and their death described as a noble sacrifice to spare the rest of us that fearful moment. Meanwhile behind the lines, women and children are being raped, dying of violence and malnutrition, and their pain and their deaths go unrecorded and unhonored.

The assumption that is made by the war slogan is that if you kill them first, you will live. (I assure you that, with the body messages I've been getting lately, I won't.) This assumption would not be possible if the daily deaths of ordinary people were made visible, and if the life process of dying were in our heads instead of the single event, and if the bravery of the old who face death every day were recognized for the courage it demands of the human spirit.

Consider for a moment the old woman, the bag lady who lives on the streets and in the doorways of New York—who not only faces death each day because of her age, her poor health and lack of medical care, but who in addition risks every night the possibility of a violent attack, rape, or murder. Contrast her situation with the man in the foxhole, who will be relieved by another man in a few hours, who is dressed in the best combat clothes our tax money will buy, who is provided the best medical care and the best diet in the world, and who knows if he is disabled, he will be pensioned for the rest of his life, and if he is killed he will have a military funeral. If we honor the old woman for the courage she shows every day of her life, there is just no way we can glorify the guy in the foxhole. And he is going to be a lot harder to recruit if the glory of dying has to be shared with old women.

In "The Power of the Old Woman" I said that I didn't have any special wisdom that comes with age to give to those who are younger. But in writing this afterword, I begin to see that I may have, and if I have, so have all the other old women. For us to pass that knowledge on, we have to break yet one more barrier of silence, the silence of the old. We have to hear that silence as political, and know that just beneath all imposed silences lies power.

I close these essays on aging with one I wrote in November of 1981. Caught between my own need to record my life experience and the silence I felt imposed on me, it was never sent out for publication. I hope the writing of this book has broken that silence and has made a place, not only for me, but for all old women to write or to talk about the bodily experience of aging.

Cambridge, 1981

Yesterday, I went to the eye surgeon to find out about a cataract in my left eye. It wasn't the first time I had gone to his office. I've been living with this cataract for about seven or eight years. The first doctor, who thought he saw it but wasn't sure, was an Asian doctor who was just learning English. He struggled to impart information to an American woman who knew little about the eye, and as I view her now, not much about life, and almost nothing about aging. Today, I know more.

For one thing, I can explain cataracts. In the eye is a clear lens, round like the eye itself, and you can see through it as you look out through your pupil. A cataract can grow quietly on the side of the lens for months, years even. (Sometimes it has felt to me as though this cataract had a life of its own—haphazard, indifferent to my life and my needs.) But as long as it does not grow toward the pupil, even though it grows slowly and grows larger, you may still look, unhindered, out at the world until the day you die and never know that for half your lifetime it lurked there. Like most things, it may grow unevenly; sometimes its growth is outward toward the periphery of the eye, sometimes inward toward the center. But if it reaches the pupil, tiny though it is—a speck—it becomes a dark cloud covering everything, shuts out word, and bird, and tree, and sky. I have sometimes imagined it something like the Incredible Hulk.

When I went to the doctor in Cambridge two years ago, he saw the cataract plainly growing at the very edge of the center of the lens. He said the cataract might grow away from the pupil or it might quite suddenly grow into the pupil. It could happen in a few months or it could take a year. He also saw one growing in my right eye. When he told me, I thought of it as a foreign object in my eye and like any cinder, I wanted it out. But when I learned it was attached to the lens of my eye and that to remove the intruder meant removing one of the lenses of the only eyes I will ever have, I took (no pun intended) a new view of the offending object.

Now it was not the vague possibility that had nagged me for eight years. It was here. It had moved in and I wondered how.

When had I so lowered my defenses as to let the enemy in? My body has been a fine body for sixty-eight years, always on my side. Even at times when I thought it, or some part of it, was my enemy—still it protected me. A splinter festered and then was out; a burn weeped, crusted, became a scar that today I cannot find; a bone splintered, and the swelling became a cast until the bone healed; germs forced their entrance, and my body burned them out with fever.

I recalled that just a few months before, the dermatologist removed a small skin cancer on my temple and explained to me that I was "older," my skin thinner; my face had had too many years of exposure to the sun; that I would need to protect it from now on. Again, I wondered how this could be. My skin had always protected me; it burned and peeled and new skin replaced the old; it tanned, it freckled—always managed somehow to shut out the sun. It had been my armor against so many things.

But I still had the possibility that the cataract could grow away from my pupil, and I could handle the simple knowledge that my skin couldn't keep out the sun. My body was still on my side; I could afford to help it along with a #15 skin protection, and still feel my body's loyalty.

Yesterday, I went back to the doctor. I walked past the trees in front of his office where, two years ago, I could still distinguish the male cardinal from his less colorful mate, could see that a mockingbird had decided to stay the winter. But walking along the Cambridge streets this time, I was less sure. This time the doctor was not certain how much longer I would see with my left eye as the cataract was growing into the pupil. He seemed defeated by a process in which he was not in charge. I felt the same defeat, as I was not in charge, either.

I left the doctor's office enraged at my fate—that something so small, a speck, actually, could alter my life as I knew this would. I felt betrayed by my own body that had always protected me. I could protect myself from the sun's rays that came from without, but this was coming from within. My body made this cataract, was making it now, and I could not stop it. My body was not only not taking care of me; it no longer knew how to operate the whole internal, unseen, magical show any more. For the first time in my life, I was afraid of it. It still had all the power it ever had, but now the power was not on my side: it had the power to make a cataract, power that could be used against me. I was suddenly frightened by all the years ahead in which I would have to live in a body that had gone amuck.

By the time I reached the car, and probably out of a feeling of fear and loneliness, I began again to feel that my body belonged to me, that it was all I had, and that together we would have to see it all through.

Today, gradually, sometimes not easily, I begin to understand that my body is still in charge of my life process and has always been. It is still taking good care of me, but it has always had two jobs: to make sure that I live and to make sure that I die. All my life it has been as busy with my dying as my living.

I'm not saying that I am not biased on the side of living and that I won't try to alter my body's plan with my own strong will; I intend to. Probably, in a few years (if I'm lucky) I will have to have surgery and have the lenses of my eyes removed to remove the cataracts. But meanwhile, I'm playing for time—all the time I can get. If I had to have the surgery done now, they would replace my lens with a plastic one, but there is risk in that. I might see fine, but with time the plastic lens could possibly cause blindness, which is irreparable: I would be blind for life. But I remember when contact lenses were plastic and hard, and now they are soft and gelatinous. So I figure, I'll take my chances and stall for all the time I can get. If they can make a contact lens soft, they can replace the inner lens with a soft one. I'm convinced that the medical world is going to devise a softer lens, not because doctors are so humane or are so devoted to the needs of the old—but for two other good reasons. Modern medicine is getting older, and that means more doctors are facing cataract surgery themselves; and the other reason is that there will be so many of us—cataract surgery is going to be big business.

I figure technology owes me something. It's ruined my drinking water, the air I breathe, the food I eat—the least it can do is give me my vision till I die. It owes me that. On the other hand, it is not my will that will decide how much time remains for me to see—my body is in charge; it knows a lot. It breathes the air, it takes in the water, it tries to build with the food from contaminated soil, and it may already know how, in the years ahead, my view of the outer world may not be as good for me, as regenerative, as I now think it will. And with the deep knowledge with which it has always protected me—now, even against my will, it turns my sights toward an inner world, more to be relied upon, more of my own making, restorative, inviolate.

Barbara's Preface to the Expanded Edition

The essays of mine that follow are in a different voice, not because I am a different woman, but because of everything that came after the publication of *Look Me in the Eye*.

I am a very private person, and I wrote those earlier essays out of my own anger and my need to expose the oppression I felt. I hoped, too, that other old women could examine their own life experiences and together we could change our lives in creative ways.

What I could not know in the late '70s and early '80s was how rapidly the scene was about to change against which ageism was to be examined. For example, the march I described in "Look Me in the Eye" was to be almost the last radical Take Back the Night march that would involve 5000 angry women. Feminists were burning out. They needed a respite, but also, as they moved towards middle age in the Reagan years, they needed less marginal incomes. Many entered mainstream jobs that required very different use of their energies and time.

Into that void moved a system for interpreting women's lives, a system that seemed to have just been waiting—the "helping professions." These were fields that had always been open to women and appeared to offer less alienated work than other jobs. But the cost was, as it had always been, the control of women's political anger through "helping" and "curing." My "Open Letter to the Women's Movement" was only a premonition of the burgeoning of services to the old. And I began to see that the therapizing of feminism that followed the second wave would continue to depoliticize every rise of feminism in the future if there were not an examination of the training in the helping professions and a recognition of its political use.

Meanwhile, Congress had awakened to the greying of America and made federal monies available for research and services to the old. They did not do so with any agenda of equality for old women. But now, with funds available, every discipline—medicine, psychiatry, social work, sociology—wanted a piece of "old."

Shortly after *Look Me in the Eye* was published, letters began to fill our rural mailbox from professional women in their thirties, forties, and fifties—gerontologists, psychologists, social workers, social scientists, therapists, and Ph.D. candidates. With no sensitivity to ageism, they were developing services, wanting data for surveys, wanting names of old lesbians for their studies, anthologies, films. I expressed my concern but they persisted, making it clear that they were unwilling to allow old women to define our own issues, to have that precious chance to know ourselves, to name ourselves, before others described us.

The work of uncovering any oppression soon brings you up sharply against the institutions that have held it in place for so long. I began to see that the obstacles to examining ageism had their source in the university system that trained these women. On the one hand stood the faculties of the established graduate schools, which are responsible for the certification of practitioners in the helping professions and whose curricula had scarcely been touched by feminism. On the other stood Women's Studies, designed and brought into the universities by feminists whose radical vision did not include old women.

I could see that old women would not be able to change our lives in creative ways unless we had some space that was not pre-empted by professionalism. I was going to have to develop a more public voice. We left our life on the desert—described by Cynthia in *Desert Years*—and I began to speak often to women's organizations connected to such institutions as social work, medicine, the university system.

Two of these talks are included here, as well as Cynthia's essay "The Politics of Beauty," and a talk given at the First West Coast Conference of Old Lesbians in 1987, the first conference ever held to claim the word "old."

I welcome the opportunity of this introduction to let go of that public voice. With relief I can now tell you something of what it has been like for my private self, how often I was uncomfortable as I found myself speaking out against ageism as a feminist while the second wave was winding down.

I hung in because I had to, for myself and other old women. Sometimes I felt as if all I had to justify my presence was a piece of the truth. As women grew weary of confrontation with each other, I felt they must be saying, "Not another oppression!" Often I felt out of step, as words like "patriarchy" became trite and other feminists were beginning to talk of the second wave as history. Sometimes I felt the voice of my own internalized ageism taking over—the fear that, in my refusal to quit the radical struggle, I would be seen as passé, not "with it" any more, a woman so old that she could not even comprehend that the movement had come and gone without her knowing. But that was not all.

I felt painfully the fact that I was raising the issue of ageism at a time when racism was a priority on the feminist agenda, and rightfully so. It was difficult for me to stand on the platform with women of color and know that the only reason there was any space for me there at all was because women of color had fought to break through the limits of the women's movement and had created such space.

But I have also felt an urgency, not only to speak for myself and other old women, but to make sure that ageism is understood by those women who, in large numbers, were the young feminists of the '70s. For when they leave the work force in their sixties, ageism will be for them a glass ceiling and a soundproof room if they do not understand that it is a political scenario. Not only will they be robbed of twenty or more of the most powerful years of their lives, but the course of feminism will be robbed of those twenty years as well. Ageism assures that young women, bonded with the fathers, will have no communication with old women who are outside the system and who could disclose the hidden lies of generations of men in power. Only the knowledge of the politics of ageism can break that bonding.

Feminists of the second wave have uncovered the many ways that men have divided women—by race, class, by looks, by able-bodiedness—and feminists are breaking down those barriers.

What we have not understood is that the separation of women by age is critical. It means that every future wave of feminism will end and another have to begin in ignorance.

But if those with experience are not silenced, I believe that when feminists have had this respite, and therapy has lost its hype, our energy will again rise with our anger. We will hear again the voices of radical women standing together in solidarity to fight for change, and the voices of radical old women will surely be heard among them.

Outside the Sisterhood: Ageism in Women's Studies

Barbara

I wish I could say with pride that I was asked to speak on ageism at the National Women's Studies Association conference in 1985, but actually I wasn't. I was asked to hold a workshop on aging. But I had put my head in the door of enough sparsely attended workshops on aging to know that I was not about to add to the trivializing of the issue of ageism. Just as feminists had fought to drive a wedge into the closed university system to admit Women's Studies in the '70s, I had to fight to get ageism included in the Women's Studies curriculum in the '80s. I told them I would talk to the entire conference body or not at all. The committee responded by inviting me to speak and, in doing so, acknowledged ageism to be a serious feminist issue.

I have not come here out of the National Women's Studies Association's spontaneous commitment to and concern about ageism. I am here after a four-year fight, after other old women along with me wrote to the NWSA planning committee and demanded that ageism be addressed at a plenary session. We insisted that

NWSA confront the question of how it is possible that the last 30 years of women's lives have been ignored in Women's Studies. This morning I have twenty minutes to speak to that topic.

I am not going to talk to you today about organizing. Old women do organize. That organizing ranges from a lobby watch of 132 women in a Detroit housing project to protect themselves from male violence, to the Older Women's League of 12,000 women throughout the United States who work to make legislative changes that affect the economic oppression of old women. But today I want to talk about what is *not* there, because until we see how invisible the lives of old women are, and why, we can not even begin the kind of radical change that the challenge of feminism demands.

From the beginning of this wave of the women's movement, from the beginning of Women's Studies, the message has gone out to those of us over 60 that your "sisterhood" does not include us, that those of you who are younger see us as men see us—that is, as women who used to be women but aren't any more. You do not see us in our present lives. You do not identify with our issues. You exploit us; you patronize us; you stereotype us. But most of all, you ignore us.

Has it never occurred to younger women activists as you organize around "women's issues" that old women are raped, that old women are battered, that old women are poor, that old women perform unpaid work in and out of the home, that old women are exploited by male medical practitioners, that old women are in jail and are political prisoners, that old women have to deal with racism, classism, homophobia, anti-Semitism? I open your feminist publications and not once have I read of any group of younger women enraged or marching or organizing legal support because of anything that happened to an old woman. I have to read the Los Angeles *Times* or *Ageing International* to find out what's happening to the women of my generation, and the news is not good. I have to read these papers to find out that old women worldwide are the poorest of the poor, or that in this country old women are the largest adult poverty group, or that 44 percent of old Black women are poor. It is mainstream media that speaks about the battering of old women, about the conditions in public housing for the elderly—in which almost all of the residents are women—or about old women in nursing homes serving as guinea pigs for experimental drugs, a practice forbidden years ago for prison inmates.

But activists are not alone in their ageism. Has it never occurred to those of you in Women's Studies, as you ignore the meaning and the politics of the lives of women beyond our reproductive years, that this is male thinking? Has it never occurred to you, as you build feminist theory, that ageism is a central feminist issue?

I look at the indexes of recent textbooks—on women and economics, on women and unpaid work, on women and psychology, on images of women in literature, on Black women, on working-class women, on women and violence—and I find nothing under "old" or "aging."

Read those books used in Women's Studies as an old woman reads them. They discuss the socialization of little girls from the moment of birth, the struggles of women through adulthood—and it turns out that "adulthood" ends with menopause or perhaps with some attention to the woman in her fifties who is a displaced homemaker. Well, just try being an 85-year-old Black woman in a shantytown in L.A. trying to cross the street when a government economic index has valued your life at only $236 should you be killed (in contrast to $328,475 for a 34-year-old white man)—try that for a displaced homemaker. But we are not women to you; we are not even adults. We are as invisible and as irrelevant in your classrooms as we are in a hostile male world—a world where we fight not only the same oppressions younger women do, but the oppression of ageism, as well, and all without the support of the women's movement.

Meanwhile, as the numbers of old women rapidly increase, the young women you taught five years ago are now working in the helping professions as gerontologists and social workers because the jobs are there. They still call themselves feminists but, lacking any kind of feminist analysis of women's aging from your classrooms, they are defining old women as needy, simple-minded, and helpless—definitions that correlate conveniently with the services they intend to provide and the salaries they have in mind. All this week on this campus, workshops on aging have been going on under the auspices of the Institute on Aging. Because ageism is not addressed, these workshops will do nothing to end the oppression of old women and will do much that contributes to that oppression. Women's Studies has not done its homework sufficiently on its own ageism so that it can begin to effect change in the academic community to stop this.

But it is worse than that. For you yourselves—activists and academicians—do not hesitate to exploit us. We take in the fact that you come to us for "oral histories," for your own agendas, to learn *your* feminist or lesbian or working-class or ethnic histories, with not the slightest interest in *our* present struggles as old women. You come to us to fill in some much-needed data for a thesis, to justify a grant for some "service" for old women which you plan to direct, or you come to get material for a biography of our friends and lovers. But you do not come as equals, not with any knowledge of who we are or what our issues may be. You come to old women who have been serving young women for a lifetime and ask to be served one more time, and then you cover up your embarrassment as you depart by saying that you felt as though we were your grandmother or your mother or your aunt. And no one in the sisterhood criticizes you for such acts.

But let me say it to you clearly: we are not your mothers, your grandmothers, or your aunts. And we will never build a true women's movement until we can organize together as equals, woman to woman, without the burden of these family roles.

Mother. Grandmother. Aunt. It should come as no surprise to us that ageism has its roots in the patriarchal family. But here I encounter a problem. In the four years it took to get NWSA to address ageism, feminism has moved from a position in which we recognized that family is a building block of patriarchy, the place where sexist, hierarchical roles are learned, where the socialization of girls takes place, the unit by which women are colonized, manipulated, controlled, and punished for infraction. From that basic tenet of feminist theory, both mainstream and radical feminists have moved back to a position of reaffirming the family. Mainstream feminists are buying the notion that as long as a woman has a "career," family is a safe and wholesome place to be. Radical feminists have affirmed family as the source of our cultures—as a way of understanding our strengths and our oppressions as Black, Jewish, Hispanic, Asian-American, Native American, working-class women. This return to family is reflected in our writings, where less and less is Father seen as an oppressor, but more as another family member, oppressed by white male imperialism. *(And, believe me, he is oppressed.)*

It will be for future feminist historians to explain how it was that, in our return to family, we never questioned its contradictions to our earlier feminist theory. Not that we can't contradict our own feminist beliefs—they aren't written in concrete—just that we never acknowledged the contradiction.

Nor can history fail to note that our return to family coincides with a reactionary administration's push back to family values, any more than it can ignore that our lesbian baby boom coincides with Reagan's baby boom to save the Gross National Product.

If we are to understand ageism, we have no choice but to bring family again under the lens of a feminist politic. In the past we examined the father as oppressor, we examined his oppression of the mother and the daughters, and in great detail we examined the mother as oppressor of the daughters. What has never come under the feminist lens is the daughters' oppression of the mother—a woman who, by definition, is older than we are.

The source of your ageism, the reason you see older women as there to serve you, comes from family. It was in patriarchal family that you learned that Mother is there to serve you, her child; that serving you is her purpose in life. This is not woman's definition of motherhood. This is man's definition of motherhood, a male myth enforced in family and which you still believe—to your peril and mine. It infantilizes you and it erases me.

This myth of motherhood is not a white American phenomenon, though nowhere, I believe, is it as bad as in white imperialist culture. Barbara Christian, in her book *Black Feminist Criticism*, points out how this myth is uncovered in the fiction of Alice Walker writing about Afro-American life and by Buchi Emecheta writing about Ibuza life. This myth is summed up by the Ibuza saying: *The joy of being a mother is the joy of giving all to your children*. It is internalized by the young mother, but then internalized and perpetuated by her daughters. So that even when—as in Emecheta's *The Joys of Motherhood*—the mother has come to some insight, her daughter continues to see her as existing only for self-sacrifice.

The old woman is at the other end of that motherhood myth. She has no personhood, no desires, or value of her own. She must not fight for her own issues—if she fights at all, it must be for "future generations." Her greatest joy is seen as giving all to her grandchildren. And to the extent that she no longer directly serves a man—can no longer produce his children, is no longer sexually desirable to men—she is erased more completely as grandmother than she was as mother.

It is for these reasons, because of everything you learned in family, that you, as feminists, can continue to see the older woman as a nonperson. It is for these reasons that you believe our lives as old women are not important and that we exist only to serve you.

We have all been so infantilized in family we have never made ourselves, as daughters, accountable as oppressors of the mothers, and we should know only too well that the failure to acknowledge the oppressor in ourselves results in confused thinking and a contradictory image of those we oppress. Thus you who are younger see us either as submissive and childlike or as possessing some unidentified vague wisdom. As having more "soul" than you or as being overemotional and slightly crazy. As weak and helpless or as a pillar of strength. As "cute" and funny or as boring. As sickly sweet or dominating and difficult. You pity us or you ignore us until you are made aware of your ageism, and then you want to honor us. I don't know which is worse. None of these images has anything to do with who we are; they are the projections of the oppressor.

I have to say of Women's Studies that when you make the lives of women over 60 invisible, when you see us as your mothers and fail to examine your oppressive attitudes, you are letting the parameters of Women's Studies be defined by men—by the man in your own heads. But more than that. In the consciousness raising of the late '60s and '70s, in the contribution made to feminist theory that grew out of those years, in the development of Women's Studies that followed, we planned curricula with an entire piece omitted: that of age and the oppression of ageism. We cannot now patch up those structures in twenty minutes to cover the gaps of our ignorance. We have no choice but to go back once again, as we have had to do before, cover old ground in new ways, and rebuild this time with a wholeness that includes all women, for all the years of our lives.

—1985

So many women have asked me, since I gave this talk, "Did they hear you?" I look back over the intervening six years and I have to say, "They heard what they could."

Look Me in the Eye *is now included as a text in Women's Studies and other departments of the university. The* Women's Studies Quarterly *of Spring/Summer 1989 was on Women and Aging. The NWSA conference in 1990 gave a priority to the issue of ageism. They heard invisibility and they made old women visible.*

What they could not hear was a voice that they had never heard before, one they would not have expected to hear from a lesbian—that of the angry mother speaking with a public voice to the daughters: "You are bonded with the fathers against me, and I will not live out a white male definition of motherhood. I am not your mother, I am a woman among you. I will not give you unconditional love or sacrifice my life for you, and I hold you accountable for your oppression of me."

They could afford to hear invisibility, but it was harder to hear equality, since that concept would radically alter their lives. They had been promised by the fathers that the old woman was servant to them for life—and it will take time for women to recognize that when the mothers have freed themselves, this will free us all.

A Call for an End to Ageism in Lesbian and Gay Services

Barbara

In May of 1984, I was asked to talk to the Lesbian and Gay Freedom Democratic Caucus in Santa Cruz, at a meeting organized and attended predominantly by social service workers. I was ill-prepared to find that the other speakers were young social workers, who were describing with pride exactly the work I was criticizing in my talk. Indeed, the gay male social worker who preceded me described teaching heterosexual hospital personnel how to recognize old lesbians and gays "by the pronouns that they use, the people who come to visit them, and the pictures in their rooms." The purpose of such identification was to refer these patients to his gay services.

This is real betrayal. Old lesbians, like all lesbians, are in charge of our own lives, and we will come out when and where we please. The last place many of us would choose is flat on our back in a hospital.

I was shocked that no one in the audience was outraged. I myself did not confront him, because I had already been so critical of the kind of work the other speakers were describing that I felt obliged to end with some positive contribution, and used their hospital setting to do so.

I am a former social worker and a lesbian who is proud of our lesbian and gay history. That history identifies us as critical of the mainstream, refusing to accept its heterosexual myths, more sensitive to oppression, more willing to examine what has gone unquestioned for generations, more willing to risk breaking old molds and creating new lifestyles. I believe in that history.

Today the mainstream is coming to terms with a growing population of older citizens. We, too, are becoming aware of our own older members of the lesbian and gay community. But as we do so—and as we become gerontologists and social workers in the field of aging—it is urgent that we take stock now and ask ourselves hard questions about the services we are providing.

We have come to a "Y" in the road. The future is not preordained. We have a choice. We can continue on the road we have so bravely travelled, where we have cut a swathe through oppression and discrimination when the going was hard. With a sense of our strong difference from a straight world, we have been willing to risk the ways that have never been tried, the outcome unseen, determined only by our own vision. Or we can leave our chosen course and take a hetero-social welfare-institutionalized direction for our own aging. (Two things can be said for this direction—it is *straight* and you can see the end of it.)

It matters to me, to Cynthia, and to other lesbian feminists which way we go. The decision will alter our lives and yours. Those of you in your twenties, thirties, and forties will have to live out what is begun now. Consider that—institutions last a long time. You are never rid of them. They only reappear in a new guise.

I have been reading the appeals of straight and gay agencies for services to the old, and it pains me to see so little difference; I see instead imitation, ageism, and practices that do not reflect the values of our heritage.

Let's look at an ad from United Way. An old woman is sitting in a dark room, staring out of her window. The caption reads, *"One day you wake up old and all your friends are gone."* The ad continues: "When you're older you'll know what it's like. The countless hours alone. The phone that never rings. The children who are so busy with their own lives. You'll realize how important the work we do is...[Our agencies] provide visiting nurses. Home health care. Protective services. And maybe most important—companionship."

Nothing in this ad tells a woman she can phone a friend or speak to the neighbor across the hall—women who are 20, 40, or 60—that she can give and take support, find a common ground. The message here is that the only friends an old person should expect to have will be her same age; otherwise, what do they mean, "Someday she'll wake up and all her friends will be gone"? What are they telling me about the phone that never rings? The message is about power, who calls whom. I should not call. I should sit and wait—other people are busy.

This woman's problem is not her age; it is ageism. She is not defining herself; she is being defined by a social agency. They are not only telling her who she is and what she should expect; they are telling younger women who the old woman is and what she expects. Such stereotyping by social agencies, whether United Way or SAGE (Senior Action in a Gay Environment), affects not only the recipient of the services but the attitude of every person in our society toward aging.

Our own lesbian and gay services, without ever examining their own ageism, also explain old lesbians and gay men to the community at large, to mainstream social agencies, and to hospitals and nursing homes. And their approach influences, as I want to show, the way our gay publications view us and the way younger lesbians view us and portray us.

The following is from a letter addressed to the producers of *Gay Seniors: The Silent Pioneers*, a documentary film prepared with the consultation of SAGE.

May 27, 1983

Dear Pat Snyder:

This is in response to an article in *Gay Community News* about your appeal for financial support and for input from old lesbians for the film *Gay Seniors: The Silent Pioneers*.

As a 69-year-old lesbian, I am concerned about how your film will portray old lesbians. I am especially concerned about how your own ageism is apparently shaping the film and how it will reinforce attitudes which the lesbian and feminist communities are trying to change. Because your film will be seen by millions of people nationwide, and their singular impression of who I am will probably be a lasting one, what you are about to do affects my life and that of many other lesbians. I am all the more concerned when you say your film will "...attempt to make some generalizations about the lives of the estimated two million lesbians and gay men 65-or-more years old."

Work [is] being done by the lesbian community to put a halt to the social work-welfare-philanthropic approach to old lesbians, perpetuated by some younger lesbians and specifically by SAGE, which is advising you in producing your film. That approach is painfully clear in the way your film is described, and I have no assurance that its content will be any different:

> *The Silent Pioneers* will examine many legal, socio-psychological, and political problems that straight society creates for older lesbians or gay men, such as denial of hospital visitation rights to non-related couples and battles over the wills of lesbians and gay men who bequeath possessions to their lovers. Many have also had to cope in silence with loneliness and bereavement after the loss of a life-long companion.

The article continues with a quote from the co-chair of the board of SAGE:

> We are very excited about the potential of this film to raise public awareness about the unique problems and concerns of older gays.

Surely you know that these "unique problems" are the problems of every gay in this country. If you ask a 30-year-old lesbian whether she's concerned, when she enters a hospital, that her lover can be denied visitation rights, she'll say, "Damn right, I am." She might even tell you an experience in which she or her lover had been refused such rights. The problem for the young lesbian may be compounded by the fact that she has parents who have never accepted who she is and who are hostile to her lover, who can move in and affirm their "rights" to visitation, consultation with doctors, determination of a course of treatment if she's unable to speak for herself. As for wills, SAGE itself mentions in a flyer that people of all ages need wills. And do you believe that, across the country, in rural areas and in many cities, young lesbians are not today facing the loss of a lover with nobody to tell about it? *It is dishonest, ageist, and exploitative to have these battles and forms of oppression projected as unique to old lesbians—to have the battles fought on the turf of the old.*

It is especially exploitative because old women are already stereotyped as powerless and pathetic. We are already seen, ad nauseum, as the embodiment of younger people's fear and shame around sickness, need, physical weakness, death, and loss of loved ones—as if these were our principal attributes, and as if they were unique to us. Must we continue to be portrayed as powerless and pathetic because that is how younger lesbians choose to see us? Or because it serves the purposes of younger lesbians?

Instead of selecting out old lesbians and gay men to ask how we feel about our "unique problems" around hospitals, wills, or the loss of loved ones, how about asking us "How do you feel about being patronized by younger people, gay or straight?" If

SAGE is to be used as a model for services across the country, if they are to advise film-makers about the lives of old lesbians, they need to start asking such questions. Or better yet, asking themselves, "How would I feel?"

SAGE circulates a reprint of a newspaper description of their services from the *Daily News*, April 6, 1982, regarding their young volunteers:

> One such volunteer is Liza, a young lesbian in her twenties who visits an infirm 80-year-old lesbian who has been confined to a hospital. "She is an important part of my life," Liza said of her older friend. "She has so much knowledge, experience, and wisdom—she's like a treasure. She's like my own collected history—it's like seeing pictures from the 1920s."

This kind of sentimentalizing and fossilizing of old women is so offensive that when I think of this woman being subjected to it I am appalled. I am compelled to try to get the entire lesbian community to wake up to our own ageism and stop this exploitation of old women. Stop it and stop it now.

I am confirmed in my fears about the film by your title, *The Silent Pioneers*. We are all pioneers; why are old lesbians the "silent" ones? Why project closetedness onto us as if—again—it were our unique problem? There are still, today, and with good reason, more "silent" young lesbians than out lesbians. To imply otherwise is classist and racist, since being out is far more difficult when you already have other strikes against you. Even the young lesbian who works on a lesbian publication or makes a lesbian film may well be closeted, "silent," on her straight job, or with her neighbors, or with her family, or when she is in a court of law, or in a hospital. The number of younger lesbians who are out to everybody everywhere is still minuscule. "Silent" is not the adjective that sums up my life to me, or the lives of the lesbians I have known.

The world has not seen many images of old lesbians and I insist that your film portray us as the real, strong women we are. I felt good about seeing *The Word is Out*. That film was not touted as "examining many legal, socio-psychological, and political problems that straight society creates for lesbians and gay men." It wasn't a film made by a social service agency about their clients. It didn't define lesbians as victims or define our problems for us. With the framework you've publicized for *The Silent Pioneers*, how will you set up interviews that elicit power rather than victimization? Will old lesbians in your film be able to say, "I *chose* not to marry, I *chose* not to raise children for the male state, and I am sick and tired of being thought of as a grandmother by straight and lesbian young people alike!" If not, I'd rather see the strong, straight old women from OWL, the Older Women's League, saying, "We're fed up with how we're treated," than be objectified by my lesbian sisters of SAGE.

I am not an enemy of SAGE. I don't want them to quit. I want them to get going. Since their beginning in 1978, knowledge of the politics of growing old has exploded before us, and I recognize that it is harder for an institution to change than for individuals. But it is imperative that they re-evaluate their program in the process of making this film, or they will turn back the clock for the feminist community and will, sooner or later, suffer the consequences themselves.

I do not want to be critical of you when you are putting out good energy without offering some positive suggestions. I am sure SAGE is deeply committed to this task and will remain so. My proposal is not that they lessen their contribution but that you broaden the base of your consultation. [I then suggested women to contact and closed the letter.]

Following the writing of this letter to the film-makers of *The Silent Pioneers*, Cynthia and I went to the Second National Conference on Lesbian and Gay Aging in June of 1983. We found not one workshop on ageism, and ageism was not even discussed as a problem. What we did find were career people looking for and talking about "them." We found a division into the able and the needy, into the gerontological community and those they view as "the isolated and lonely." We found a few old lesbians and gay men caught up again in serving the young. Like Liza, the SAGE volunteer who saw the old woman's life "like pictures from the 1920s," old lesbians and gay men were asked over and over to "tell us how it was": objectified and fossilized for the benefit of the young. We found a duplicate of the traditional, heterosexual-social welfare-philanthropic approach, administered by gays and lesbians to be practiced on old gays.

As a final example, this March I received a second, revised questionnaire, a survey of lesbians over 60, from CERES (Center for Research and Education on Sexuality). The ageism in the original questionnaire had prompted my "Open Letter to the Women's Movement." The revision made changes in the most glaringly ageist language: they no longer described old lesbians as living in "self-imposed isolation," or as "lonely and depressed," and they no longer described those receiving their services as "having their problems solved and their accomplishments recognized by an appropriate service organization." But the thrust is identical in the two questionnaires. This is not a questionnaire to find out who old lesbians really are. It is geared to establishing a population for service agencies, and its results will go to social service agencies nationwide, both lesbian and straight.

It should be obvious that unless this questionnaire is sent to lesbians of all ages, the results will tell us nothing about old lesbians as having any particular need that younger lesbians do not have. But the ageist presumptions and the social service bias result in questions the responses to which are guaranteed to indicate special needs. Let me give you just one example (Question 15):

How do you feel about participating in each of the following?

- ❍ Social Organization for Older Lesbians Only
- ❍ Social Organization for Older Lesbians/Gays
- ❍ Social Organization for Older Women
- ❍ Social Organization for Older Women/Men

No one asks you how you feel about social segregation by age. There is no category for Other. The question itself clearly informs me where I might belong and where I do not belong. I do not belong in an age-mixed group unless the younger people are paid to be there.

Throughout our lives, lesbians and gay men have developed enormously creative ways of living by refusing the mainstream values. And now, at the end of our lives, gerontologists and others of the established helping professions want to push us into conventional, patch-up, disempowering social services, while they use us to accomplish what they can't accomplish for themselves. As if somehow, around 60, we had lost that lifelong capacity for creativity and now want nothing more than to rejoin the heterosexual family model—what SAGE proudly calls its "family setting"—and play "Grandma" and "Grandpa" to our gay, salaried children. This is not only ageism, this is homophobia. This is not equality.

Those of us who are lesbian or gay and in the helping professions have inherited two histories—our proud gay heritage on the one hand, but also a history of psychiatry, psychology, and social work practiced on women and gay men that is an embarrassment to us today and leaves us much to be accountable for. I see no way we can develop lesbian and gay services unless we root out the ageism, sexism, and homophobia built into our training.

It is time, not just for SAGE or other agencies to raise their consciousness about ageism, but for all of us to work on this together. Not the able helper and the needy recipient, but together in a relationship of equality. Equality demands that we empower each other, and you do not empower if you do not look at the source of the oppression. To empower is to politicize. Equality demands that we who are old have the power to name ourselves. I do not want United Way or the geriatric community, gay or straight, to name me.

I have been critical. You may well ask, "What then do you envision?" I leave you with one example that can stand for many others: your hospital services. Let representatives of the entire lesbian and gay community, old and young, go as a committee to confront the medical community and root out the homophobia in our hospitals. Don't tell them *my* story because I am old—let every one of us in our twenties and forties and eighties tell our own experiences in hospitals. A 30-year-old lesbian's story is no different from mine. Don't hide behind the false "respectability" of "our elders," or the false pity either—that is, don't hide behind ageism to get the job done.

When that job has been done, every admissions room in every hospital will have, in plain view, the telephone number that any one of us of any age can call to reach the Lesbian and Gay Hospital Task Force. And in learning to work together, as equals, we will have begun the long, hard job of ending ageism.

—1984

Ageism and the Politics of Beauty

Cynthia

I wrote this after sending several letters to feminist publications, protesting the depiction of old women in their artwork and their fiction. Among other forms of ageism, younger women were still using a stereotypical language of revulsion—"deterioration" and "ravage"—to describe old women's bodies. In this essay, I wanted to question why these insults seemed acceptable.

If you are a younger woman, try to imagine what everything in society tells you not to imagine: that you are a woman in your seventies, eighties, nineties, or older, and yet you are still you. Even your body is yours. It is not, however, in the language of the embalmers, "well-preserved," and though the male world gives you troubles for it, you like it that way. Apart from those troubles, you find sometimes a mysterious integrity, a deep connection to life, that comes to you from having belonged to a body that has been large and small, thin and fat, with breasts and hips of many different sizes and shapes, and skin of different textures.

In your fifties and sixties when your eyebrows and pubic hair and the hair on your head began to thin, it bothered you at first. But then you remembered times when you tweezed your eyebrows, shaved your pubic hair and legs and underarms, or took thinning shears to your head. "Too much" hair, "too little" hair—now you know that both are male messages.

One day you pick up a book that you find rich and nourishing, published by a feminist press. It is a political book and a sensuous book, and you like the way its politics and its sensuality seem merged. One of the authors is a poet in her fifties, with a warmth of connection to other people, especially women. It is when you come to a section about aging that abruptly the connection—with you—is broken. You find the poet writing with dread and loathing at the thought that one day she must live inside the body of a woman who looks like you.

Stop!
I don't want my scalp
shining through a few thin hairs.
Don't want my neck skin to hang—
neglected cobweb—in the corner of my chin.
Stop![1]

It shouldn't take this guided tour for any of us to recognize that an old woman must find it insulting, painful, personally humiliating, to be told in print that other women in her community find her body disgusting.

What you—the old woman—find especially painful is that the feminist newspaper where this excerpt was first printed, the feminist publisher, the poet herself, would surely protest if Jewish features, Black features, or the features of any other marginalized group were described—whether in the form of the outsider's contempt or the insider's self-hatred—with this kind of revulsion. They would not think of their protest as censorship of literary expression. They would know that such attitudes do deep damage to a work artistically, as well as humanly and politically.

Yet clearly there are not the same standards about speaking with disgust about the bodies of old women. So the message has a double sting. The "ugliness" of your physical being is not a cruel opinion but an accepted fact; you have not even the right to be insulted. How is it that you, the old woman, find yourself in this place?

I believe the revulsion towards old bodies is only in part a fear of death, as the poet suggests—she ends the poem, "*No quiero morir.*" (Of course there is no reason why women over 60 should have to hear such insults whether they remind us of death or not.) Or else everybody would find soldiers going to battle repugnant, young women with leukemia disgusting, the tubercular Violetta in *La Traviata* loathsome. This is a death-obsessed and death-fearing society, that's true enough. But the dying *young* woman has always been a turn-on.

No, there is another more deeply anti-woman source for this disgust. Once again it is men who have defined our consciousness and, as Susan Sontag noted ten years ago, in aging as in so much else a double standard reigns. True, old men who are quite powerless are sometimes viewed by younger men *as if* they were old women. But old men routinely seek out much younger women for erotic companions and usually find them. In white Western society, the old woman is distasteful to men because she is such a long way from their ideal of flattering virginal inexperience. But also she outlives them, persists in living when she no longer serves them as wife and mother, and if they cannot make her into Grandma, she is—like the lesbian—that monstrous woman who has her own private reasons for living apart from pleasing men. On the one hand she is a throwaway, on the other a threat.

White men have provided the world with little literature, sculpture, or painting in which the old woman's body is seen through the eyes of desire, admiration, love, wonder, playfulness, tenderness. Instead they have filled our minds with an extensive literature and imagery of disgust, which includes a kind of voyeuristic fascination with what they see as the obscenity of female aging. Men's disgust for old women's bodies, with its language of contempt (shriveled, sagging, drooping, wizened, ravaged, liver spots, crow's feet, old bag, etc.) is so familiar to us that it feels like home.

Still, if this were all, how is it that twenty years of ground-breaking feminism have not led us to rise up to challenge such a transparent, gross form of woman-hating? An honest answer to that question is painful but essential, and Barbara Macdonald has named the key to our resistance. Younger women can no longer afford to ignore the fact that we learned early on to pride ourselves on our distance from, and our superiority to, old women.

While I was thinking about this article, the picture of an old woman caught my eye from the comic pages. The three frames of "The Wizard of Id" show an old woman with thin hair pulled to a tiny topknot on her head, her breasts and hips a single balloon. The Wizard, her jaunty old husband, hand debonairly on hip, legs crossed with a flair, has bragged: "The king and I are judging a beauty contest tonight." She wags her finger. "That's degrading!" she exclaims through her down-turned, toothless mouth. "My lady friends and I will picket!" The Wizard gets in the last word, which of course leaves her speechless: "That'll make a nice contrast."

This slice of mainstream media is jammed with political messages. Old women are ugly. Their view of things can be dismissed as just a way of venting their envy of young women. The old men, who have status and power, and therefore are the judges who matter, prize the young women's beauty and judge old women's bodies to be contemptible. The old woman has no defense since she, too, knows old women are ugly. And: the young woman's body in fact gains in value when set beside that of an old woman.

Images like this accustom younger women to unthinkingly adopting an ageist stance and woman-hating language from men. But also the old woman's low currency temporarily drives up our own. Just as the "plain" white woman is at least not Black, the "plainest" younger woman is at least not old. The system gives us a vested interest in maintaining the politics of beauty and in joining in the oppression of old women.

The principal source of the distaste for old women's bodies should be perfectly familiar. It is very similar to the distaste anti-Semites feel toward Jews, homophobes feel toward lesbians and gays, racists toward Blacks—the drawing back of the oppressor from the physical being of the oppressed. This physical revulsion travels deep; it is like fear. It feels entirely "natural" to the oppressor; he/she believes that everybody who claims to feel differently is simply hiding it out of politeness or cowardice.

When I was twelve, I had an argument with my grandmother. (Because of ageism, I feel a need to point out that she was no more racist than most white Baltimoreans of all ages in the 1940s.) It was probably my first political argument, and I felt both shaky and strong. Buttressed by a book on what in the '40s was called "tolerance," I didn't see why little Black girls couldn't go to my school. I can still remember her voice as she bypassed the intelligence argument. "But just think—would you want one to come to your house and spend the night?" *Yes, but would you want to marry one?* Physical revulsion is an ideal tool for maintaining oppressive systems, an instant check whenever reason or simple fairness starts to lead us onto more liberal paths.

To treat old women's minds as inconsequential or unstable is in one sense more serious, more dangerous, than disgust for their bodies. But most women find that the more our bodies are perceived as old, the more our minds are dismissed as irrelevant.

And if we are more than our bodies (whatever that means), we also *are* our bodies. If you find my body disgusting, no promises that you admire or love my mind can assure me that I can trust you.

No, the issue of "beauty" and "ugliness" is not frivolous. I think of two white women who are in their sixties. One, a lesbian psychologist from a working-class, radical home, has written about the compelling urge she felt to have a facelift—until she became aware that what she was dealing with was not her own ugliness but the ugly projections of others, and became instead an activist against ageism. The other, a former airplane pilot and now a powerful photographer, has made a series of self-portraits that document, mercilessly, the bruises and scars of her own facelift. These are not conforming Nancy Reagans. These are creative, independent, gutsy women, and they heard the message of society quite accurately: the pain of an operation for passing is less than the pain of enduring other people's withdrawal.

One example of how the danger increases when an old woman's body is seen as less valuable than a younger woman's is that the old woman is unlikely to receive equal treatment from medical practitioners, male or female. Old women attest to this fact. Recent research agrees: a UCLA study confirms that old women with breast cancer are treated less thoroughly than younger women, so that their lives are "needlessly shortened."

In her pamphlet, *Ageism in the Lesbian Community* (Crossing Press), Baba Copper points to the daily erosions of "ugly." She observes that the withdrawal of eroticism between women "which takes place after middle age (or at the point when a woman no longer passes for young) *includes withdrawal of the emotional work which women do to keep the flow of social interactions going:* teasing, touching, remembering details, checking back, supporting" (emphasis mine).

I hear a voice: "All of this may be true. But aren't you trying to place the heavy boot of political correctness on the mysteries of attraction?" No. But obviously the fewer women we can be drawn to because they are "too" Jewish or fat or Asian or old, the more impoverished our lives. And also: if we can never feel that mysterious attraction bubbling up towards an old woman, a disabled woman, an Hispanic woman, we can pretty well suspect that we are oppressive to such women in other ways.

Sometimes I sense a presumption that the fact that each of us is growing older gives us all license to speak of old women's bodies in insulting and degrading ways—or even makes this particular form of woman-hating somehow admirable and honest. Yet the fact that one of us may well in the next twenty years become disabled or fat doesn't make feminist editors eager to hear the details of any "honest" loathing we may feel for the bodies of disabled or fat women.

It does not surprise me that ageism is still with us, since eradicating oppressive attitudes is hard, ongoing, embarrassing, painful, gut work. But as a movement we have developed many sensitivities that are at least well beyond those of the mainstream. And we are quite familiar by now with the basic dynamics that almost all oppressions have in common (most of which we learned from the insights of the civil rights movement and applied to feminism and other liberation movements). Erasure. Stereotyping. Internalized self-hatred, including passing when possible. The attempt to prove the oppression is "natural." Impugning of the mental and emotional capacities. Blame-the-victim. Patronizing. Tokenizing. Segregation. Contempt mingled with fear. And physical revulsion. So it seems almost incredible that we have not learned to identify these most flagrant signals of ageism.

How can we begin to change? We—especially those of us in our forties and fifties—can stop the trend of examining in public how disgusted we are at the thought of the bodily changes of growing old. Such examinations do not display our moral courage. They reveal our insensitivity to old women who have to hear once more that we think their bodies are the pits. We can recognize that ideas of beauty are socialized into us and that yes, Virginia, we *can* begin to move in the direction of re-socializing ourselves. We can work, for ourselves and for any revolution we might imagine, to develop a deeper and more resonant—dare I say more *mature*—concept of beauty.

I am looking at two photographs. One is of Septima Clark, on the back of the book she wrote in her late eighties about her early and ongoing work in the civil rights movement. The other is a postcard of Georgia O'Keeffe from a photo taken twenty years before her death. The hairs on their scalps are no longer a mass, but stand out singly. O'Keeffe's nose is "too" strong, Clark's is "too" broad. O'Keeffe's skin is "wizened," Clark's is "too" dark. Our task is to learn: not to look insultingly beyond these features to souls we can celebrate, but instead to take in these bodies as part of these souls—exciting, individual, beautiful.

—1988

Note

[1]The poem excerpted here is "Old," by Rosario Morales, from *Getting Home Alive* by Aurora Levins Morales and Rosario Morales (Firebrand Books, 141 The Commons, Ithaca, NY 14850, 1986), p.188.

A Movement of Old Lesbians

Barbara

The First West Coast Conference of Old Lesbians in June, 1987, is best described by the brochure that was mailed across the country: "Our purpose in calling together old Lesbians, 60 and over, is to explore who we are, name our oppression, celebrate all that we represent, and make our presence a force in the women's movement." What it does not reveal is the agony the planning committe went through in claiming the word "old." It does not reveal the weeks of work that finally resulted in limiting attendance to lesbians 60 years old and over. Nor does it reveal the anger of younger women at the decision which excluded them—an anger which continues today as old lesbians build a political movement.

It is important to understand the resistance of younger women to such an act. It was not that 50-year-old women were eager to call themselves "old," or that 30- and 40-year-old women longed for our company. In 1987, when white middle-class feminists were sentimentalizing crones, foremothers, and "our elders," to hold a national conference in which old lesbians shut out the daughters was unthinkable. We were defying a tenet of male-defined family which younger women have assumed to be a fact all their lives: that the older woman is not subject, but servant. It was shock that kept younger women at the door.

We have come together for the first time as old lesbians to examine ageism and its impact on our lives. Many of you may ask why, in the face of so much violence against old women in the mainstream, does this conference focus on ageism in the feminist and lesbian community? Why do we accuse our sisters? Why don't we focus on ageism in the white male society that we rub elbows with every day? I want to suggest an answer to that question.

Because we *are* the lesbian feminist community. And we won't recognize ageism until we recognize it in ourselves, just as we could not address sexism in the larger community until we had uncovered the effects of sexism in our own lives. Ageism coming from our peers hurts more. Ageism in the straight world is no surprise—there is no shock, it is no contradiction to their fundamental mainstream beliefs about women, and it serves their goals well. But ageism in our own feminist community does shock us. It is such a contradiction to feminism, to our own beliefs about women, and it does not serve our vision of a new society.

Let me give just a couple of examples to remind us of the invisibility of old women in our community. A friend of mine set out one day to find her way in a new city. She stopped a younger dyke and asked her, "Could you tell me where the lesbian bars are and where women go to dance?" The younger lesbian looked at her blankly and said, "We go to the Sisterhood Bar just down the street to dance, but I don't know any bars for *old* lesbians." My friend, after recovering from the shock, responded with appropriate anger, "Look, I didn't ask to marry you—I just asked where dykes meet and dance."

Or take *Plexus*, for more than a dozen years the newspaper of the women's movement in San Francisco and beyond. Here is how it advertised itself in the *Women's Yellow Pages:* "The award-winning national newspaper that has been reaching 18-to-54-year-old women for eleven years." I regret the recent demise of *Plexus*, but I have to recognize that it is a newspaper that took pride in announcing it was not for me or for you.

But we meet an additional obstacle in organizing to end this invisibility. For, like the young woman who didn't know about bars for old lesbians, or the editors of *Plexus*, we come from family and carry our dread of old women with us.

We have become the old women we dreaded to be, and we all know how odd that experience is. We are the women we once saw as boring. We are the women we didn't want to look at. We are the women we expected should sit on the sidelines always loving and admiring us. And we are the women we were once told we must have "respect" for, this admonition to prevent our taunting, our jeers, our ignoring—to prevent our showing contempt for old women.

As long as we hold onto this legacy of our own ageism, we oppress ourselves from within. But I believe that every one of us can most—or part—of the time separate ourselves from our internalized ageism. At such times, we know that we are seen as ugly and we know that we are not ugly, only old. We look at ourselves and watch our bodies change with a sense of wonder and know we are in step with life. We see that young women expect us to give them unconditional love, to step aside for their lives which we are expected to acknowledge are more important than our own, and we are angry at this childish expectation. We hear the young woman's words on the way to the bar and we know she is the same young woman who would say she has respect for old women. We know we will not settle for honor or respect and the contempt these words cover up. *We will not settle for less than equality.*

We have become the old women we dreaded to be; we find we like being who we are now and live it with joy. We have come here to celebrate it.

And yet there is still a dread that holds us back from taking charge of our lesbian power. What is it then that we dread? Is it not some unnamed fear of the future—something that keeps moving ahead of us but is never where we are? Doesn't the 60-year-old say, "I like being 60, but what will happen when I'm 70?" And doesn't the 70-year-old say, "Being 70 is exciting, but I don't know what I'll do when I'm 80?" And doesn't the 90-year-old enjoy 90 and worry about being 95, 96, or 97 and beyond?

Isn't it true that we come to each of these plateaus of age and we look around for that thing we dreaded and say, "It isn't here yet—it must be something that comes later." And when we reach the next plateau, we look around and say, "It isn't here—yet—it must come later."

Are we not dealing with a myth of old age—an accumulated deposit of everyone's fears of the uncertainty of life, which all of society has pushed ahead each year until it is compressed into the farthest end of our lives? And we, who are old, are expected to live out everyone's fear—not of old age—but everyone's fear of the uncertainty of life itself.

There is an urgency in calling this conference at this particular time in feminist history because we need to look at what, in our own community, feeds and perpetuates this fear of our future.

As all of you are aware, services have been developed by lesbian professionals, primarily younger women, to assume the role of loving protectors of us—to use their words, "their elders." They are segregating and stereotyping us in ways that are a replica of mainstream services and that are disempowering to us individually and to the movement of old lesbians to eliminate ageism.

We need a dialogue with these services. For in the mainstream such services perpetuate ageism, ghettoize, discourage political organizing, and set up a welfare-model approach to women's old age. In the straight world such a model suits a male agenda. Transporting these services into the lesbian community—without criticism, without any analysis of ageism—means we are being asked to accept separate-but-equal and allows professionals to explain us to the world.

We are being named before we can name ourselves by women who feel they have the right to name us whether or not we choose. In professional journals we are described in patronizing tones. And our own publications—having no awareness of ageism—feature these descriptions of our childlike simplicity, our neurotic fears, our gratitude for their goodness, as the latest word on lesbian aging. Such descriptions feed a panic about old age that already is given prominence by younger lesbians and feminists in fiction, essays, and poetry.

I read an essay by a lesbian in her fifties, writing in a lesbian quarterly of her terror at someday being my age. Another woman, also in her fifties, describes her horror that someday she will have wrinkles, sagging breasts, a croaking voice. One is a sensitive and sophisticated dyke; the other a brave and politically radical straight feminist. They are among the best of the lesbian and feminist community. Yet each tells me the revulsion with which she experiences me. Neither of them sees the ageism in this panic. As Baba Copper has pointed out, we have to assume that they must not imagine we are even reading their words.

I know of no other group in our community who is so blatantly patronized, made the subject of others' revulsion, pity or sentimentality, and who is also so openly exploited by professionalism.

Our own panic about what's ahead leaves us undefended from such ageism. In that panic lies the power we give to the younger professional lesbians to take control of our lives. In that panic we can be tamed into asking nothing for ourselves in the present—not making demands to be seen and heard and valued right now, but instead to timidly ask only that someone rescue us from our imagined and dreaded future selves.

Some of you may be thinking, "But living in a wheelchair, being paralyzed from a stroke, unable to hear or see, or being unable to speak, these are inherent risks of old age." But they are not inherent risks of old age—they are inherent risks of life, which any of us may face at any age, any day of our lives.

As we confront the problem of segregating and patronizing services, surely we have a model of autonomy in the movement of disabled lesbians and disabled straight feminists who are challenging the women's movement.

These are women, some of whom struggle for each breath, are severely disabled by a stroke, are palsied, or move about in wheelchairs. They have not asked of the women's movement that some dyke be assigned by an agency to come to their home to talk about lesbianism because they are lonely; they have not asked for separate housing or separate centers for the disabled. They have not been segregated into separate tea-dances for disabled women.

They are demanding that their needs be met by the larger women's community in a spirit of equality—and we should learn from them and form coalitions with them as we develop an autonomous movement of old lesbians.

What kind of a movement will ours be?

As lesbians, we have a lot on our side. Aging and ageism can only be defined outside of family. In patriarchy, the old woman has always been defined as grandmother. Nobody even knows how to think of old women outside of the grandmother role. Who is in a better position to examine both the oppression of ageism and the reality of women's aging than old dykes? We have not taken the well-marked route from daughter to wife to mother to grandmother, adjusting our behavior to fit a series of male definitions of who we should be at each stage. Somewhere along that track we each said no.

Oppressions are uncovered by the group most affected—those who daily feel the oppression, whose lives are chipped away by each encounter. Until one day one woman, and then another, decides, "No more. I will not ignore this hatred, I will not try to run away from it, I will not collude with it. I will search it out willfully, deliberately—whether it is disguised as deference, honor, respect, or sympathy, or whether it presents itself as naked hatred of my aging body or as a primitive fear of my old and ancient rage."

Having made such a commitment, the task is not going to be an easy one. We will be seen as "harping," "obsessed," "divisive," "carping," and "vicious." Our efforts will be seen as singular, quirky. Unlike other oppressions that have already been named, there is not a body of accumulated work to document our experience. No visibility of a 300-year-long and continuing struggle to get out from under the yoke of exploitation in America; no written account of 2000 years of worldwide oppression to name what we feel; no first wave, no second wave of anti-ageism to make us a part of a sisterhood that will bear testimony to our experience. We will be divided into the angry old woman and the one who does it right, who is tokenized. We will feel very much alone, and women we may have called "sister" in other struggles will separate from us and deny our reality in this one.

But let this be a movement of brave old dykes led by brave old dykes. Age is a time of great wonder—a time when we have to hold, with a fine balance, contradictory truths in our heads and give them equal weight: old is scary but very exciting, chaotic but self-integrating, narrowing yet wider, weaker yet stronger than ever before.

It is we who must name the processes of our own aging. But just as we could not begin to say what it means to be a woman until we had confronted the distortions of sexism and homophobia, we cannot explore our aging without examining and confronting ageism. It is the task that lies before us.

—1987

spinsters book company

Spinsters Book Company was founded in 1978 to produce vital books for diverse women's communities. Today Spinsters is one of the largest lesbian and feminist publishing companies in the country.

Spinsters is committed to publishing works outside the scope of mainstream commercial publishers: books that not only name crucial issues in women's lives, but more importantly encourage change and growth; books that help to make the best in our lives more possible. We sponsor an annual Lesbian Fiction Contest for the best lesbian novel each year. And we are particularly interested in creative works by lesbians.

If you would like to know about other books we produce, or our Fiction Contest, write or phone us for a free catalogue. You can buy books directly from us. We can also supply you with the name of a bookstore close to you that stocks our books. We accept phone orders with Visa or Mastercard.

Spinsters Book Company
P.O. Box 410687
San Francisco, CA 94141
415-558-9586